FU-FU-FU-FRANK!

One Man's Struggle With Tourette Syndrome

BY FRANK BONIFAS

authorHOUSE®

AuthorHouse™
1663 Liberty Drive
Bloomington, IN 47403
www.authorhouse.com
Phone: 1-800-839-8640

First published by AuthorHouse 11/17/2010

ISBN: 978-1-4520-6802-2 (sc)
ISBN: 978-1-4520-6803-9 (e)

Printed in the United States of America

This book is printed on acid-free paper.

2012

Enjoy!

Frank J. Bomfas

Dedication

This book is dedicated to my parents, Jim and Rita Bonifas, whose lives became upended when Tourette Syndrome invaded our family. I can never thank them enough for supporting me throughout my life.

Acknowledgments

Recognizing every person who has helped me over the years is impossible, so rather than risk offending anyone, or creating a list longer than this book, I profoundly thank each individual who has shown generosity and understanding to me. You have given me the hope that it takes to confront all the adversities I face.

Maladie Des Tics

The symptoms of Tourette Syndrome, (TS) were first recorded in 1825 by a French physician who observed a young noblewoman introducing obscene words into her ordinary conversation. However, it would be over a half century before it was again recognized by a young Parisian neurologist, George Gilles Tourette, who selected the case as an example of the illness that he classified as "maladie des tics." Several decades passed before it again appeared, without determination about whether the disease was psychosomatic or organic in origin. Various explanations were cited as to the reasons for these tics. Some insisted that they were a manifestation of hysteria, or resulted from bad habits developed during childhood. Many felt they developed from repressed familial psychological conflicts or a repressed libido. Other studies found that their existence had organic explanations. A great number of people were convinced that anyone with the bizarre symptoms of TS had to be possessed by the devil.

Even in 1960, after the drug Haloperidol was found to be effective in the treatment of TS, the disease was largely thought to be a psychological reaction. Finally, after the creation of the Tourette Syndrome Association in 1972, a patient support group, the disease emerged as a neurological disorder characterized by tics—involuntary, rapid, sudden movements or vocalizations—that occur repeatedly. In spite of this finding, TS is still considered to be psychosomatic by many European nations. The vocal tics of TS can be simple, such as grunting, barking, yelping, and throat clearing, to complex ones including syllables, phrases, echolalia (repeating other people's words, pelilalia (repeating one's own words), or coprolalial (obscene words). Some with TS will describe a need to complete a tic in a certain way or a certain number of times in order to relieve the urge or decrease the sensation.

The most dramatic and disabling tics include motor movements that result in self harm such as punching oneself in the face, picking at one's skin, or impulsively poking other people during conversation. When the movements involve the same muscle groups over a period of time, severe disabilities may result.

Many problems are commonly associated with TS. The two most common are obsessive compulsive disorder (OCD) and attention deficit hyper-activity disorder (ADHD). Obsessive behaviors usually begin several years after the occurrence of tics, and besides the usual need for order, arranging, counting, checking for order, etc., the compulsions manifest themselves in obsessive thoughts, some of them so bizarre that their victims never repeat them to anyone. Many of these thoughts include those of impending doom, either of themselves or of a loved one, and have a great influence on their lives. Attention deficit hyperactivity disorder is characterized by inattention, making it difficult to recall events that may have recently occurred, complete assignments, or hold a job that demands much concentration. Patients with this disorder are usually hyperactive, often on the go, as if driven by a motor. They are often impulsive, and need to interrupt conversation or await their turn.

Most of the tics experienced in TS disappear during focused activities, such as singing, playing a musical instrument, participating in a stage production, swimming, or playing a a sport. Tics usually become worse during stressful experiences, holidays, or anything causing a change in one's life.

Some victims of TS improve in the late teens and early adulthood, but about 10 percent experience a lifetime of severe symptoms. While medications prove beneficial, in many cases they lose their effectiveness after a time, and the search for relief must begin again.

Foreword

Try to imagine waking up in the morning and facing a normal day when you know that you will have no control over most of your physical and verbal actions. You want to strike up a normal conversation with a family member, friend, co-worker or new acquaintance, and before you utter a single word of what you really want to verbalize, it is preceded by a strand of stuttering and a string of obscenities usually beginning with the word "fuck".

Imagine the ultimate humiliation and extreme frustration that you would feel when these words were most definitely not what you had in your thoughts and you are unable to control their leaving your lips no matter how hard you tried to suppress them. Further, imagine constantly poking or touching the person you wish to partake in the encounter as you tried to initiate a normal conversation.

As Frank's family physician for the past 12 years, I have witnessed firsthand the torment that Frank tries desperately to cope with every day due to his illness. Tourette Syndrome in itself is an awful debilitating condition because it causes the body to react and move without the brain being able to control the behavior, and most often, even with medication, it allows the sufferer to exhibit only mild control over extremely uncontrollable and outrageous behaviors. What makes the disease most difficult to treat is that it is almost always coupled with other health problems. Obsessive compulsive disorders, hyperactivity, oversensitivity, and extreme nervousness are some of the many other problems that often coincide. In Frank's story, the reader will become quite aware that he exhibits many of these additional problems. He has what would be considered a severe case of Tourette Syndrome. It is exasperating as his doctor trying to find the combination of medication or treatment in order to help Frank lead a somewhat normal life. I have worked with many of his specialists to implement their prescribed treatments in order to try to help Frank. As one of his doctors, I can only imagine Frank's irrepressible frustration in his trying new medications and treatments with very little and often only temporary relief.

Frank lives every day struggling endlessly for any type of solution to take him from his torturous state.

Reading the story of his life, one can't even begin to imagine what his true existence must be like. Growing up in a world that had no idea what his illness was, and doubting that he was unable to control his actions, Frank was ostracized by most everyone. Although his family tried to understand and undoubtedly took great measures to help him, this often meant Frank spent a great deal of his life in mental institutions, hospitals, and experimental programs. Exorcisms were even performed to force the "demons" from his body and mind. He was abused by many who misunderstood, believing that his verbal and physical actions were able to be controlled, taking advantage of his illness. Many openly refused to empathize with his plight. Teachers, administrators, relatives, peers, clergy, and many others often added to his humiliation and torture.

Certainly, today much more is understood, and Frank's illness is identifiable. Medications are used to try to subdue some of the undesirable reactions that persist with this illness. However, there is no cure today, and those afflicted with Tourette syndrome must live with great uncertainty, often finding it to be greatly debilitating in many aspects of their life.

In his story, Frank tries to expose the difficulties in trying to lead a "normal" life. Living in Frank's world has to be incredibly exhausting. He is in constant confrontation, battling the "demons" he has no control over and losing the battle no matter how hard he tries. His daily existence, certainly, is severely limited. Working, socializing, and what should be simple daily functioning, which most of us do without contemplating, are in Frank's world daunting and many times extremely humiliating activities. As a devout Catholic with great moral values, his religion has been both a foundation to provide hope and yet, a source of great grief for transgressions that his uncontrollable condition has propelled. Frank's severe case of Tourette Syndrome makes his existence immensely painful. It is both our hope and the hope of many others who deal with this illness that knowledge and education of the condition will provide understanding and extend empathy to those suffering this disease. Perhaps, with future advancements in medicine, a total cure will be discovered.

I must comment that Frank is an amazing man. Although he battles his condition almost every day of his life, he continues to find some moments of happiness throughout his torturous journey. Perhaps, it is in his deep-seeded Catholic faith, or the supportive friends that he has made in spite of his illness. I believe that it is Frank's certain belief that beyond this earthly world he will find his deserved, ultimate peace. Learning to know Frank has given me great pleasure and my own personal frustrations. I am frustrated that I cannot successfully find the combinations of medicines or the program that would extinguish the horrible symptoms of his awful illness. The pleasure of knowing Frank is in recognizing his courage, strength, and undeniable faith that provokes him to continue in life. It takes a strong individual to be trapped in a body that will not cooperate with one's mind and force one's self to go forth. This book in itself is quite an accomplishment. It was painfully written and a difficult task to complete due to his condition. It is my hope that Frank's story, in his own words, will give others afflicted with Tourette Syndrome the same courage Frank has found to continue. I hope it will provide great insight to the illness, and in this way, others can come to understand, empathize and support those with Tourette Syndrome who desperately struggle to lead a "normal" life.

With hope,
Philip R. Masser, M.D.

∂∽∾

I first met Frank Bonifas when I had just finished my psychiatric residency and was working with Drs. Arthur and Elaine Shapiro and Dr. Richard Sweet at New York Hospital. In those days, the goal of our group was to convince the medical establishment that Tourette's syndrome (TS) had a neurological basis. The patients we were studying were almost all severely affected and most had previously been considered to have serious and incurable psychiatric disorders such as psychoses However, when one took the time to know these patients, it was apparent to us that they were not "crazy" at all—simply unfortunate people who were fighting valiantly to live normal lives despite bizarre and uncontrollable symptoms.

Since that time, more than thirty years ago, my medical practice has mostly been devoted to treating patients and doing research into this very baffling and fascinating disorder. Thanks in a large part to the Tourette Syndrome association, much research has been done and there is currently a far greater understanding of what it means to have TS. The diagnosis is made more readily and many children are helped significantly with medication, family education, and therapy. In addition, books and television shows have educated the public so that there is a wider understanding of the disorder. Although more medications become available all the time, none are yet directed specifically at Tourette syndrome and while Tourette syndrome is primarily a children's disorder, there are a number of people who continue to suffer from it all of their lives and who do not respond to or cannot tolerate any of the medications currently available. Frank is one of these unfortunate people. I have always known Frank to be a kind, considerate and sensitive person who has struggled daily with a condition that has forced him to be isolated and, too many times has made him the butt of cruel jokes.

This book will give the reader some idea of what it means to suffer from lifelong TS. However, I know that the struggle has been even harder for Frank than he wants to admit. Frank's hope, and mine as well, is that many people will read this book and come away with greater insight into what it means to have Tourette syndrome.

Ruth Dowling Bruun, MD
Adjunct Associate Professor of Psychiatry (Part-time)
New York University Medical Center

I first met Frank Bonifas in February of 1973. We both had agreed to participate in a neurological research project requiring months of in-patient hospitalization at New York Hospital-Cornell Medical Center. Frank and I endured much during this time in our lives. First, we both had, and still do have, very severe cases of Tourette Syndrome, and second, these research projects were rather primitive in design and did not take into account the potential suffering of the participants. Thus, we were abruptly taken off the medications we had been on for a long time. Then we were very quickly brought up to very high doses of the research medication they were studying, and after roughly one month, the medication was abruptly discontinued only to start another round of the trial medication. Frank and I went through hell on these protocols, enduring all types of side effects, such as insomnia, severe akathisia (motor restlessness), mood swings and Parkinsonian symptoms, including marked bradykinesia (slowing of movements), to name a few. My ability to move became so compromised that my brother would have to come and feed me because I could not move my cutlery. It was as if my upper extremities were paralyzed. We both were hospitalized for many months. I turned 16 while a patient there and Frank was 19 at the time. Because of this nightmarish ordeal we had endured together at New York Hospital in pursuit of a "cure" for our malady, we bonded in our suffering and became close. To this day we remain in contact.

I became fascinated with the field of medicine when I was a senior in high school largely as a result of what I had been through as a patient. So I entered New York University in the fall of 1975 as an incoming freshman. I became extremely dedicated to my dream of becoming a doctor despite most people around me believing it was merely a fantasy. Despite my severe Tourette and the associated problems I had with reading, I did well in college and was accepted into medical school in May of 1981 at New York Medical College. After a grueling four years I was accepted into an internship at Yale-New Haven Hospital in Pathology. The following year I transferred to Mt. Sinai Medical Center in New York City for a residency in Biological Psychiatry. I completed this successfully and proceeded to embark on a Fellowship also at Mt. Sinai Medical center and the Bronx Veterans Administration Medical Center in Consultation/Liaison Psychiatry. I finished my training in June of 1990. I then became Board Certified and a Diplomate the following year of the American Board of Psychiatry and Neurology. After considering various professional opportunities, my wife and I relocated to Frederick, Maryland in 1990, where I became Medical Director of Psychiatry at Frederick Memorial Hospital. For many years I have practiced psycho pharmacology in Frederick and nearby Hagerstown. Over the years I have treated many patients with Tourette Syndrome and other neuropsychiatric disorders.

I believe that my medical background, training in neuro-psychopharmacology and my experience as a Tourette patient has had a positive effect on Frank. Frank lives in a small community in Ohio and relies heavily on his local family doctor to treat his Tourette..

Unfortunately, usually someone with a case of Tourette as severe as Frank's requires the expertise of a specialist. What I have happily done over the years is provided Frank's physician with guidance in managing Frank's Tourette. I believe that Frank and I have both grown as a result of our relationship and we have been a source of support for each other in coping with Tourette Syndrome.

Orrin Palmer, MD/Frederick, Maryland

A Faithful Advocate

We first met Frank through our daughter who was dating a young man from Coldwater, a small town about seven miles south of Celina where we live. She came home one night, telling me about the boy who "barked." I had no idea what she meant, but she said he made weird noises and the kids teased him constantly. Well, being a young working mother, I was busy with my own life, preparing for my daughter's college years, facing the fact that she would be leaving home, so I didn't think much more about this kid of whom she had spoken. My life went on quite well, thank you, without cluttering it up with people outside my small circle of family and friends. HOWEVER!!! Although she was no longer dating the same boy, she kept in touch with Frank, and one day she invited him over to meet us. Thus Frank Bonifas entered our lives. Frank was extremely nervous at our first meeting. Our daughter had asked him for lunch, and he was trying so hard to be on his best behavior. As I was soon to discover, when he is nervous, he shouts and curses. This shocked me, as I had never been exposed to anything even close to what I was hearing. I tried to cover up how I felt, but I believe Frank understood. He asked if he could play our piano. I was skeptical of his ability to play, but I said he could go ahead and give it a try. To my astonishment, he played beautifully, and no tics came out of his mouth while he played. I truthfully did not understand what

I was hearing. Later I was to learn that many people who suffer from this syndrome are very musical indeed. At any rate, we invited Frank back and he has been an inspiration in the lives of each of my family members. Because she had been exposed to someone with Tourette Syndrome, my other daughter, a school teacher, was immediately able to see that one of her small students was exhibiting these symptoms. She called the family of this student for a conference, and spoke with them about her fears. They immediately scheduled an appointment with a doctor who diagnosed the child with Tourette Syndrome, and he was able to get early treatment for the disease..The parents were extremely grateful for the understanding she had shown to their family. All because of Frank! Frank was not so lucky. Years ago when he began suffering from those tics, no one knew what caused them, and they just thought he was crazy! Well, all the time he spent in psych. wards was about enough to make him doubt his own sanity. In his mind, he felt sure that he was mentally all right, but just couldn't figure out why everything was so uncontrollable.

Understanding Tourette Syndrome is not easy. Since it is a neurological disease, we should be able to treat it, right? There are so many drugs out there, and some of them have helped in some way or another, but for the most part, Frank has been a guinea pig. Many drugs have been tried, but to get the exact drug and the exact dosage that will control his tics without making him almost zombie-like, has been challenging for all the doctors who have been involved. Too little, and his tics run rampant; too much, and he can barely move. The inconsistencies in the drug dosage have affected his mind, and he has terrible thoughts running through his head. Much of the time it's hard for him to tell real from unreal.

We have seen Frank through good times and bad. He enrolled in Wright State Lake College after high school, and many days after finishing class, he would stop by our house to sleep before he felt capable enough to drive the rest of the way home. He knew where we kept the key, and I told him to use it whenever he needed. Many times I would come home from work to find him asleep on our couch. Thoughts of suicide are always just below the surface, and he spoke of this to me throughout our friendship. I have shared many tears with Frank, but we have also had a lot of laughs. He has a great sense of humor, but most people aren't willing to get close enough to see it. The few friends he has, have been absolutely staunch in their relationship and have upheld him in every way. The bank for which he now works is to be commended for their wonderful treatment of this outstanding young man. Frank strives for the best in his work, and gives the job all that he has. The disease and drugs have taken such a toll on him that he is unable to hold a full time job. He worries constantly that his best is not good enough.

Frank comes from a solid background of German Catholics. His family and his community are very rigid in their beliefs, and Frank has this deeply imbed-ded in his mind. He is totally faithful to God, at one time thinking that he would enter the seminary. It is extremely difficult for him to reconcile his Tourette's to a loving God. Sometimes he feels it is a harsh God which he serves, and he wonders at times how to keep the faith. Sometimes I wonder that, too. His family has been to hell and back. I honestly can't imagine liv-ing every day of my life with a Tourette Syndrome vic-tim. At one time years ago, he said to me, "Why can't my mother just take my tics for granted, and not get all upset with me? My tics don't seem to bother you. You never point them out or say anything about them. That's how I want my mom to be. I said,,"Frank, all I have to do is put up with your tics for a few hours at a time. I don't have to live with Tourette Syndrome. You are not my responsibility. That's why your tics don't bother me. When you leave, my life goes on, but your mom will live with Tourette's every day of her life, just as you do."

But of course Frank's tics have bothered me, as they do everyone who comes in contact with him; I have just learned to accept them as part of who he is. One cannot be with him very long before it begins. A finger punching your shoulder, his foot kicking at your foot, tossing his head, shouting his favorite curse, or starting a sentence which he has to keep repeating over and over before he can get all the words out. He is absolutely unable to control these things. Frank not only has Tourette Syndrome, but has every aspect of it that is possible. Some Tourette sufferers lead almost normal lives because their symptoms are so slight (maybe a rapid blinking of the eyes, a tightening of the throat, a small head jerk, something you would not especially notice if you were not aware of this syndrome). Some of these people are on little or very light medication. They lead full, productive lives. They marry and have children. Frank has every symptom this terrible disease can throw at him, and he is still standing. He has an unshakable belief in God, but his belief in his fellow-man is fragile. He has seen the worst that people have to offer, but then out of the blue, someone will be exceedingly kind to him. With the writing of this book, he has unleashed his demons. We will never know the full extent of those demons. Please read this book, and become more tolerant of those who are not like you, or those you don't understand, because this life could be your life.

This is Frank's story.

Wilma Kuenning

Author's Remarks

I am truly sorry if some of the obscenities in this book are alarming to its readers, but without them, one would never really fathom how repulsive Tourette Syndrome can be. All of the events described are true, and have occurred in spite of my unbounded faith in God . As you read my story, please think of them as symptoms of TS with all its complications that I have no control over.

Frank

Chapter 1

When I was in the seventh grade, the strange thoughts began. I remember looking up at the steeple on the church and thinking, "The Blessed Virgin is a f...er!" I'll never know what prompted that thought, and did not even know the meaning of the word, but I did know that it was obscene. I knew for sure that by having that thought, I was destined to be condemned to hell for eternity. The incident occurred one day when I was hanging out at my dad's gas station. I had just finished a discussion about the Catholic Church with one of the salesmen who was a regular caller at the station. I don't recall the content of our discussion, but no matter how hard I tried, attempts to forget the ensuing thought were unsuccessful. It has been many years since that episode, but I'm still remorseful for that obscenity, and will never forget it.

As I rode my bike all that summer, the thought reoccurred and I closed my eyes trying to erase it. This led to several collisions with parked cars and numerous bruises, but I obtained no relief from the obsession. Similar thoughts bothered me both day and night. I was certain that the devil possessed my mind, and would say to myself, "In the name of Jesus Christ, begone! Stay away!" I began cursing the devil for all my problems, and felt that he had to be at fault. No God would permit such thoughts to plague anyone! In later years I learned that those thoughts were from a disorder called OCD, short for obsessive compulsive disorder, commonly found in anyone afflicted with Tourette Syndrome. Dressing in the morning had to be done in the proper sequence; washing my hair had a certain pattern; brushing my teeth entailed a series with the exact number of times on one side followed by the same ritual over my entire mouth. In my thoughts, any deviation from that order would produce disastrous results, such as death, severe injury, or other consequences.

I was born in Coldwater, Ohio, into a family with deep Catholic roots. Dad's brother was a priest and his sister a nun. When I was young, Father Cap and Sister Dulcina (later, Sister Catherine) were my idols, so I planned to follow in my uncle's footsteps and join the priesthood. Coldwater is located in Mercer County in the western part of the state. The area is predominantly rolling farmland, and in the spring of the year before the corn has grown, you can see miles and miles of farm buildings that look much like those on a monopoly board. The scenery is dotted with numerous small towns that are populated largely by Roman Catholics. Nearly every town has at least one saloon and one Catholic church. The churches have all withstood the passing years and are an important part of the community. I suppose the same can be said for most of the saloons (with the exception of a few additions, subtractions and name changes on the shingles).

When traveling on State Route #127 in Mercer County, you'll undoubtedly see an impressive dome capped building with a large gold cross at its summit. Completed in 1922, it was once a thriving seminary of learning for many young men studying to be priests or brothers and was known as Saint Charles Seminary. The structure houses a beautiful chapel called the Chapel of the Assumption that was completely renovated in 1960 and is a pleasure to see.

In 1969 as vocations to the priesthood declined, the seminarians, along with those from the religious communities, were incorporated into other theological institutions forcing the school to close. It then became simply Saint Charles, and provided living facilities plus an infirmary for retired priests and brothers.

St. Charles encompasses 1380 acres with a large pond used for fishing and swimming, plenty of trees, and other amenities. Until recently, eleven-hundred acres were farmed and used as pasture for a large herd of dairy cattle. This was operated by a hired herdsman and four Brothers, a title given to men who have dedicated themselves to the Church, working in any capacity when needed. Today a portion of St. Charles has been converted into a senior -citizens' independent living center and the home for retired clergy and laymen.

Several miles away in the town of Maria Stein, Ohio, you'll find the National Marian Shrine of the Holy Relics, containing authenticated vestiges of over 500 saints and martyrs, plus artifacts from Christ's life. This is the second largest collection of its type in the United States, and most of them were acquired in 1872 by the Reverend J. M. Gartner when he was visiting in Rome. At that time the churches of Rome were being plundered and robbed of these artifacts by Italian bandits who sold them to various pawnshops where they were purchased by the highest bidder. A large number of the artifacts were placed under Apostolic Custody until they could be safely redistributed among the churches.

Through a personal friend, Father Gartner acquired a collection of these precious relics for the churches in America. At the advice of other hierarchy in the Church, he obtained several valuable additions in Venice, famous for its relics. Eventually he set sail to America to find a safe haven for the preservation of these treasures.

The Convent Chapel of the Sisters of the Precious Blood at Maria Stein was chosen because of the Sisters' practice of continuous prayer before the Blessed

Sacrament. The original chapel was completed in 1875, and in 1890 the present chapel was built to enshrine the relics. It is filled with awe inspiring gold-filled altars which caused a friend of mine on his first visit to the chapel to shout, "Wow! I've never seen so much God-damned gold in my entire life!" I've been told that when I was an infant, my aunt, Sister Dulcina, envisioned a light above my head, raised me before the altars of the chapel, and proclaimed, "If this baby does not become a priest, he will be a misfit in society!" Little did she know how prophetic those words were!

I spent my early childhood doing the things that other kids did, and I probably was into as much mischief as anyone else. Mom often told the story about a trip we made to Washington, D.C. to visit my aunt and uncle. We drove two cars for comfort reasons, but also because I was a rather hyper child who made traveling difficult. After arriving at our destination, the men and women drove separate cars and took turns taking me along because I was "such a nuisance." One day as I was driving with the men, I suddenly cried, "I mell moke! (smell smoke)" As most men would do, they said, "No you don't. That's your imagination." After I continued to complain with increasing volume about "melling moke," they stopped the car, and got out to investigate. To their surprise, smoke was pouring from the hood of the car and the engine was on fire. By some coincidence, Mom and my aunt met with us a short time later, and I became the hero of the day. That ended my hearing about being such a nuisance, but I remained the typical four year old who made traveling less than enjoyable.

In the first grade I seemed to have quite a bit of talent. At Christmas time, I amazed Sister Dulcina, by dramatically telling the story of the birth of Christ to the class, using all the appropriate hand gestures and expressions. Sister was stationed at the relic chapel shrine at Maria Stein, and was so impressed that she asked me to give my presentation to the nuns at the chapel. At the end of the presentation, everyone clapped, and I received my reward of a popcorn ball and a crucifix.

Later that year our teacher started a block-band. Everyone was equipped with drum-sticks, and beat the rhythm on blocks. I was chosen to direct the band. It was my first introduction to the music world, and I loved it. My teacher told Mom that I had a definite ear for music and should develop it.

Until I was eight years old, life was fairly normal for me. I interacted socially with other children, played the usual neighborhood games, and had many friends to keep me occupied. Contact sports never appealed to me, but I was content to be an observer whenever my friends engaged in them. I did well in school and my parents were very proud of me in spite of the fact that all my report cards included "lacks sufficient self control" on them.

In the second grade a large amount of time was spent getting ready to make our first communion. Because I had quite a loud voice, I was selected, along with two or three other boys, to lead the prayers in English. I'll never forget the wondrous feeling I had from receiving the host for the first time. In later years I became an altar boy, and at that time, reached the conclusion that I was destined to become a priest. While I appreciated being a part of the magnificent ceremony of the Mass, being an altar boy was quite a challenge for me. At that time the Mass was read entirely in Latin, and we had to learn all the prayers and responses in that language. To make matters more complicated, at one part of the Mass we had to carry a large missal down the steps from the altar, and bring it back up to the other side of the altar. My greatest fear was of falling down the steps during the process. We also had to light all the candles for the Mass. It still amazes me that I never fell down those steps and burnt the church down.

I have many happy memories from this age. My Aunt Ruth, Mom's sister, brought her three children over several times a week, and while she visited with my family, we rode our bikes all over town, went swimming, and played "Mass." I was always the priest, and we used those cheesy gold fish for communion. Many times I would return to my aunt and uncle's house and stay all night.

I attended public school, but many of the classes were taught by nuns who incorporated religion into their curriculum. Most of the Protestant children attended their own classes in another building until junior high school when all classes were held in the same building.

When I reached the second -grade my problems began. For some reason I repeatedly began to throw my pencil into the air, trying to catch it. The teacher felt this distraction was a nervous habit that I would out-grow, but later, along with the pencil throwing, other noisy tics presented themselves. I would continually clear my throat when nervous, and make sounds of "umph-umph-g-g-g-g-g—c-c-c-c" with other disturbing noises.

All of those actions were becoming most disturbing in my classes, so my parents took me to a pediatrician. After a thorough physical and neurological exam the doctor told my parents, "There's nothing wrong with this kid." To me he said, "You don't want to be a mouse, do you, Frankie?" When I answered no, he said, "Then quit making those sounds and throwing your pencil into the air." He also advised Mom and Dad to have more children. Today that solution would not even be considered, but at that time my behavior was simply viewed as unacceptable. The answer to such conduct was discipline, and having another child was supposed to cure me of such attention-seeking devices. Since producing a sibling on short notice was impossible, my parents bought a dog for me. They paid fifty dollars for a full-blooded dachshund named Corky. That was high price to pay for a dog, and not long ago an acquaintance of my parents told me that she thought I was a very spoiled child for Dad and Mom to spend that much money on an animal.

Corky and I became great friends, but unfortunately he was hit by a car and killed six months later. As any child would be, I was devastated, and it was a long time before we had another pet.

I spent quite a bit of time playing at Dad's gas station and his business lured many salesmen to the establishment. Unfortunately, more than one of them had lasting effects on me. One day one of the men approached me when I was by the air pump, grabbed both me and the air hose, and discharged the air from the pump down the front of my pants. This of course really frightened me, and then he asked, "Do you ever play with yourself?" I answered, "Sure, I play the organ, swim, read, and ride my bike." He said, "No, you don't understand. How do you play?" I replied, "I play with my cousins and the neighbors, and we play different games." He gave me an odd look, and asked more questions that didn't get the proper response from me, so he left.

The following year Dad, Mom, Grandma Miller and I took a train trip across the country to visit Dad's two sisters in California. Before we began our trip, I told Mom that I was afraid that we'd never make it back to Ohio. I was certain we'd be knifed or something. This was another manifestation of the OCD that had begun, and would continue the rest of my life.

It didn't help matters that the first train we boarded was a dilapidated pile of old metal and steel. Thank the Lord, our second train was beautiful, and had the name El Capitan. Our trip took five days and nights, and though it was completely uneventful, we witnessed some remarkable scenery along the way. Not all of it was good, as the train route also took us through some of the worst parts of the country, causing us to realize how fortunate we were for all that we had.

On arrival we were met by our relatives, and experienced some great times. We visited Disneyland and my favorite place, San Juan Capistrano, where the swallows return the same date every spring. It was a beautiful place, with the most awesome altar I had ever seen. We then went to San Diego and visited Dad's other sister. Even Dad enjoyed that trip, and we were all a little reluctant to leave when it was time to go home.

Chapter II

Throughout the lower grades I was plagued with a lack of coordination, and was always chosen last for the ball team (a definite sign that you were a klutz). Our park sponsored what they called Peewee leagues for the very young boys, so I tried to participate in those games. Every time I'd be up to bat, one of the boys, (the same one every time) would yell, "Everyone come in! Blue-Bonnet's up! He strikes out every time!" In Peewee ball it's hard to strike out because they usually throw the ball to you until they hit your bat, but for some reason that kid must have felt better putting me down. The parents usually attended those ball games, and most of them sat together. Mom joined them, and because she always felt good if one of the boys hit the ball, she would cheer for him even if he were a member of the opposing team. Some of the women yelled at Mom for doing this, saying, "You're not supposed to cheer for those kids." The same parents would call to their children, "You'd better get on base or you won't get any supper!"

Being able to excel in a sport was so important because it meant being accepted by one's peers, something everyone of that age desires. To make matters worse, I had to get glasses, and the nickname "four-eyes" further contributed to my feelings of inferiority.

Fortunately, my Aunt Ludvena convinced my mom that I should pursue my musical talents, so Dad and Mom purchased a five-hundred dollar Lowry organ and I began lessons. My teacher was Mrs. Sauer, and we traveled to Ft. Recovery weekly for sessions. I did fine at first with no trouble reading the notes, and I thoroughly enjoyed the experience. I played the organ for hours at a time without manifesting one tic. This phenomenon remains to this day whenever I engage in any musical activity. From what I have read, this is a common occurrence in Tourette Syndrome and its related diseases. I've never heard a good explanation for this, but it occurs most often when one is engaged in concentrating on a task.

My fourth grade teacher in school was Miss Kathy Liddy, and I immediately developed a crush on her. She was a new teacher who was very vibrant and quite a change from the nuns who taught us previously. She was not as strict and always open to new ideas. I remember her teaching the class a new song at Christmas, "Do You Hear What I Hear?" It is still my favorite Christmas carol. After she was in Coldwater for a while, she expressed some dissatisfaction with living here, as there was not much to do in a small town. This was most upsetting to all of her students, so you can imagine our delight when she announced her plans to get married to a Coldwater man. She married Jack Schenking in April of that year, and lived here until her death a few years ago.

Kathy was teaching the year that President Kennedy was killed. Most people remember what they were doing upon hearing the news, and I recall making igloos out of clay at the time. After the announcement of his death over the intercom, Kathy led us in praying the rosary, even though we were in a public school.

When I was in the fifth grade I was summoned to the hallway of my classroom to meet with my dad. With tears of joy in his eyes, he announced that my sister Teresa was born. She was such a welcome addition to our family, a beautiful baby, and loved by all of us. I suppose her perfection led me to become quite jealous of her, as I was feeling more and more inadequate at the time.

Shortly after Teresa's birth my mother was hospitalized with postpartum depression. With no specific medications for the illness, a long recuperation was required. With the help of family and friends, she eventually recovered. I'll never forget her friend Anne Jackson coming over and physically placing Mom's hands into pie dough and shaping it into a crust, helping her overcome her lethargy.

At that time, Father Cap was managing the St. Charles Seminary. With that position came the responsibility of saying daily Mass at Mercy Hospital and distributing Holy Communion to the patients. All of this occurred very early in the morning before breakfast was served, and the patients were wakened and draped with a sheet awaiting the arrival of the priest. Since it was difficult for the patients to stay awake until he appeared, I was chosen to accompany him, ringing a small bell to herald his arrival. There was a little nun in charge of all these arrangements, and she used to say to me, "Frankie, I know that you really love Jesus, and want everyone to know that he is coming, but please don't ring the bell so loud. Some of these patients are too sick, and you'll disturb them."

Afterward, Father was offered a breakfast fit for a king, but most of the time he elected to come to our house, wake my mother, and have her make his morning meal. He would also sleep at our house to avoid the drive from the seminary to the hospital every day. This practice continued until the priest in charge learned that he was not staying at the seminary. To our relief the practice stopped and Mom got some rest.

In January of 1965 Father Cap became associate pastor at St. Agnes Church in the Pacific Province in Los Angeles, California. He welcomed this assignment because the climate permitted him to "play golf and tennis every day." Dad and Grandma Miller flew to California in 1968 to join in the celebration of the 25th anniversary of his priesthood. Everyone had a great time, as Dad's other two sisters, Lucille and Joan, were already established there. Grandma stayed for the summer to help Dad's sister, Joan, who was expecting her first child.

That same year Father Cap developed respiratory problems, and when it became difficult to run his huge parish, he took the job of being the chaplain in a youth prison in Manteca, in northern California. He remained there until his retirement in early 1990. He seemed to do very well there, and was a genius at fixing the residents' radios and televisions.

At that time many ecumenical changes were occurring in the Catholic Church. Latin was no longer the exclusive language of the Mass, and more emphasis was being placed on removing religion from our public schools. Nuns no longer wore their habits, and it was quite a surprise when contrary to our belief that they shaved their heads after taking their vows, they emerged with full heads of hair.

I often stayed after school helping the nuns clean the class room and grade papers. Our conversations periodically drifted toward the changes in the church and the Catholic religion in general. One day I was informed that I was no longer needed after school. Apparently one of the custodians had overheard our discussions and issued a complaint that such talk should not be allowed in a public school. This incident ended my hobby of making rosaries in school when we couldn't go out for recess because of bad weather.

In the seventh grade my vocalizations were in full swing, barking, snorting, sniffing, hissing, and more. These noises, coupled with the severe spasmodic jerking of my extremities, caused total disruption to all my classes, and the teachers had much trouble maintaining a learning atmosphere. Everyone seemed to have a solution about what should be done with me. We received literature about a reform school in Cincinnati, Ohio, and I quickly burned the contents and the envelope. The local chiropractor thought he could be of help; another physician suggested hypnosis. None of these therapies proved effective.

Dr. Beare, our family physician, advised my mother to be a strict disciplinarian, so one day she carried out a threat to hit me after every outburst. By the end of the day her hand was sore and she felt guilty, while my bottom was sore and my spirits were shot. Nothing was accomplished and the tics continued.

I had begun to help my dad at his business, the Bonifas Gulf Station. None of my work ever met Dad's expectations, and the day usually ended with my going home complaining to my mom.

Chapter III

Having the severe tics of Tourette Syndrome is humiliating, but the accompanying intrusive thoughts from my obsessive compulsions are damnable. This was not only trying to me, but also to my parents, as I was constantly checking to see if Dad, Mom, and Grandma were all right. My Grandma Miller was one of my best friends, so I went to live with her in her trailer to give my parents some rest. Whenever my mom doubted any of my abilities, Grandma would say, "Now, Rita, Frank is an intelligent boy. Don't worry about him."

An entire book could be written about my Grandma Miller. She was a short, feisty woman who took no nonsense from anyone. She had been married to Frank Bonifas, my name sake, and they lived in a rented house on land that they farmed. Together they reared six children, twins Casper (Cap) and Catherine,

Lucille, Jim (my father), and Joan. A son Bernard died in infancy.

In 1931, Cap left home to study for the priesthood, and the following year Catherine began her life in the convent studying to be a nun. Cap always said that since he never wanted to work on the farm and wasn't interested in dating, the priesthood was the only choice that was left for him. Dad was only 7 years old at the time, so he remembers little about the twins in their early years. In1940, when Dad was fifteen years old, Grandpa Frank died. Because there was no one else at home to help on the farm, Dad quit school to do the work. In later years Cap repeatedly ridiculed Dad for being a poor farmer who would probably never get a good job because he quit school as a freshman. I remember his telling Dad, "Someday I'll piss on your grave because you had to work so hard." He was relentless in his criticism of Dad's not having a higher education.

Some time later Grandma decided to move into town, so she sold all their livestock and equipment for seventeen-hundred dollars and hid the money under her mattress that night. She and her family purchased a home that had running water and electricity, and moved to Coldwater. Grandma liked to tell about Dad's reactions to the house. All those modern conveniences were so impressive that he spent the entire first day flushing the toilet and turning the lights on and off.

In order to support her family, Grandma rented several of the rooms in the house to single women teachers, providing them with laundry service and meals. She soon met Pete Miller, who had three children of his own. Pete was a rather quiet man with an ever present pipe in his mouth. They were married in 1943, shortly after Father Cap's ordination, and theirs was the first wedding that he presided over.

Cap was soon assigned to several parishes in Detroit, Michigan, and in the 1950's became pastor of a mission parish in North Dakota, where in winter the temperature was usually 24 or 30 degrees below zero at night. When his church burned down, Grandpa and Grandma Miller drove to North Dakota and helped the parishioners rebuild the church. They also took care of the parish house for them.

In the early 1960s Father Cap returned to Ohio to be a part of the Church's mission band. He traveled to various parishes to present sermons about Christian living to the parishioners.

When all their children had gone, Grandpa and Grandma sold their house and purchased a mobile home. After Pete's death I often stayed with Grandma. The two of us living in that trailer in such close quarters often became challenging, with Grandma yelling, "Stop that yapping!" whenever my tics became especially loud.

Because Great Grandpa Bonifas had married a gypsy woman, Grandma always claimed that the Bonifas family had gypsy blood in it. Grandma said that they were all very restless and liked to wear lots of jewelry. Every year we made a visit to the cemetery where many of the Bonifas clan were buried. I can still see Grandma bending over the plots saying, "Now where is Uncle so and so buried?" When she found the grave, she would take her cane and pound on the tombstone muttering, "There's the goldern son of a bitch! He never did amount to anything! He's probably rotting in hell now." Then she'd find the next relative and deliver a similar epithet. I'm not sure any of us got much spiritual satisfaction from those yearly visits, but the process certainly must have been cleansing for her.

In the meantime, Catherine had become Sister Dulcina, and after the reforms of Vatican II, changed her name to Sister Catherine. She was assigned teaching duties in various schools in the area, and also had the job of explaining the relics to visitors at the relic chapel in Maria Stein. I was always very frightened of her. She was soon assigned to the first grade in Minster, Ohio, and Dad, Mom, and I became frequent visitors in her classes . She liked to show us what she had taught the children. We learned that she was probably a good teacher, but very strict. On one occasion, she had the children demonstrate how she had taught them to sing the hymn, "Silent Night" in German. Sister Catherine followed Father Cap to California in 1968, and taught students at the SanLuisRey Academy. It was rather strange, as they never could get along with each other, but found it difficult to be separated.

In the spring of 1966, Becky and Pat Tangeman and I were summoned to the church's choir loft by Sister Vincentia. With a great deal of unease as to what we had done, we met her there and were pleasantly surprised when she asked us to play the organ for some of the morning Masses. We each played for two Masses a week, and at the end of the month received one dollar per Mass. Although none of us became wealthy from the endeavor, it was very enjoyable for me to perform for an hour with some purpose and not be disrupted by the symptoms of my affliction. While the job was satisfying, it became increasingly difficult to remember how to read music. With much coaching from my mom, I managed to learn some of the notes and improvise the rest by playing chords.

In 1967 Dr. Beare advised that I see a neurologist in Dayton, Ohio. The following is a report from that visit: "The patient's parents state that he makes funny noises from his throat. They become more frequent at times. Sometimes it is understandable what is said, sometimes not. The patient did not seem to know anything was going on. He does not seem to have control over them. The patient states, 'I want to stop them.' and upon communication from his parents, at times he does seem to stop the noises. They state that he will spend as much as an hour before going to sleep at night making these noises. Sometimes they are rhythmic, sometimes they are not. It is to be

21

noted that during the interview there was one period in which the patient appeared to be looking out of the window more or less speaking to himself in a soft tone, seeming unaware of being in my presence. The patient at times has disagreements with his mother. He gets along better with his father. He resists authority to a certain extent, but is not combative. He enjoys sports, but as an observer rather than a participant. He is active at school, plays the organ at Mass, and is a Mass server. His schoolwork and grades are good. The patient does state that at home he is rather lonesome. He does not invite his friends to his house, although his mother tries to insist that he do so. He reads a lot and spends much time to himself at home. He states that he has quite a few dreams, and there is usually stuff in them.

His speech appears to be somewhat disrhythmic, and volume of the word is not always with the proper accentuation. The neurological examination otherwise appeared to be normal. There is a question to consider psychogenic phase of this behavior, and it is suggested that with continued observation, sodium dilantin be given in graduated doses increasing the weekly levels to the point where the patient feels drowsy. At a future date an EEG should be done."

Today as I read the report from that doctor, I find it very difficult to understand, as my mom was the one who encouraged me in all my endeavors. We were always very compatible, with Dad on the opposing side. Also, the school was very much aware of my problems because of the disruption in the classroom. I received an EEG in February of 1968. It showed an abnormal EEG with moderate build up in hyperventilation and numerous bursts of a generalized disrhythmia in sleep.

My parents knew that there had to be an explanation for all my symptoms, so in the spring of 1968 they made arrangements for me to be evaluated at the University Hospital in Columbus. We had to be there at two o'clock on Good Friday, which meant that I would miss all the services at church. I remember going to Mass on Holy Thursday evening, and staying afterward praying that God would take away all the sounds, grimaces, and especially the weird thoughts that I was having. When I didn't come home, Dad came to church and convinced me to leave.

When we left for the hospital on Friday morning, I was convinced that I would never see my home again. In some ways that thought was rather comforting because of all the insults and mocking I had endured from my peers. It was a beautiful day with the sun shining brightly, and when we passed the Olentangy River, I was astonished to see so many college students sun-bathing and rowing boats in the river. I said to Mom, "It's Good Friday and the boys and girls aren't in church for the three-hour services."

University Hospital seemed foreboding to me, and when we arrived at the admitting office, I was ready to run in the opposite direction. The first order of business was to put a name tag on me, stealing any anonymity I would have in this huge place.

When we got to the floor where I was to be admitted, the nurse instructed me to put on my pajamas, and gave me a small cup to pee into with instructions to clean the end of my privates with a little towel before doing so. What a strange place this was! She came in about five times asking if I had voided. Of course I replied, "No." I had no idea what voided meant and was too embarrassed to ask her about it.

After I had changed into hospital finery, my parents returned, followed by the chief physician with all his medical students. They were quite impressive in their white starched coats, and I was so frightened that the tics, sounds, and grimaces were temporarily scared out of me.

Dad and Mom stayed in a rooming house until Monday or Tuesday when they had to return to work. Dad was working at the station, and Mom worked at the switchboard at Our Lady of Mercy Hospital in Coldwater. I truthfully felt that our local hospital was the only place to be treated, as I knew everyone and they all knew me. I begged my parents to take me home with them, but they reassured me that they would be back at the end of the week.

The week was filled with their observing me, drawing much blood for tests, and doing numerous x-rays. Fortunately for me, there were two women from a nearby community on the same floor, and as we became acquainted, it helped pass the time. When they asked me why I was there, I told them that I had a brain tumor.

It was disappointing for all of us as no reason was found for my symptoms. I later learned that surgery had been suggested, but it would have been experimental and cost between 60 and 100,000 dollars. Thank goodness my parents did not have the money for the procedure, and we went home.

Chapter IV

*O*ne afternoon while my parents were at work and I was alone in the house, the doorbell rang. I was surprised to find one of Dad's salesmen at the door. He explained that he was a doctor, and thought that he could help me with my problems. Because I was desperate for help, and also thought I knew the man, I permitted him to enter. This was probably one of the worst decisions of my life, as it was the start of my first encounter with sexual abuse. After it was over, I was too ashamed to tell anyone, and when he came back on numerous occasions, I became too frightened of him to stop it. This abuse went on for a long time but stopped after I began living with Grandma in her trailer. Mom called one day with the news that "Barney" was visiting and wanted to see me. After I refused to meet with him she accused me of being very rude to the man who took such an interest in me.

I finally agreed to a short visit, and made it just that. Of course, Mom immediately felt my hostility to the man and questioned me about it after he left. It was then that I confessed to her what had been going on, and we both hugged each other while I cried until I fell asleep. Mom promptly called Dad, who wasted no time getting in touch with the salesman, and informing him in no uncertain terms that if he ever saw his face in the area again, he would see to it that he got exactly what was coming to him.

Today such action would have landed the man in jail. He would have been listed as a sexual abuser, and I would have gotten counseling to help alleviate the horrible guilt I still carry with me. I can't help thinking that it may have given me the courage to stop later abuses that occurred.

With the departure of summer, my freshman year of High School was approaching. Much of the curriculum was required, but a few selections had to be made. I opted for Spanish because the teacher was Lucy Haver, a neighbor and friend of ours. At least I would be protected for one period.

The most fearful aspect of freshman life was being initiated by the seniors, and of course, I became a prime target for some of them. One day they cornered me, forced me into a large garbage can, and rolled me all the way down the steps to the first floor. Initiation was not limited to the seniors, however, as one evening after a scavenger hunt hosted by one of the school clubs, some sophomore boys led me to an alley behind school and took my pants down saying, "Now we'll see if he is a dog or a human being." This was in reference to my barking tics which had become louder and more frequent. I didn't tell anyone about this for fear of further repercussions, but such experiences are never forgotten.

A more positive occurrence that year came from my being befriended by some senior girls. I'll never forget or be able to thank them enough for all their support. In all probability it kept me from completely losing my sanity. They treated me as a normal human being, picking me up for school, and making me a part of the activities that we participated in.

This was also the year when things began happening with my mind. It was extremely difficult to follow directions; therefore, assignments were never completed on time and I did very poorly on exams. Music lessons came to an end because of my inability to concentrate.

To make matters worse, my parents felt that I should be able to have some control over my violent outbursts, so in October of 1968, I was admitted to Upham Hall, the psychiatric ward of University Hospital. The psychiatrist assigned to me seemed very arrogant, and we had no rapport with each other. During our sessions together I sat in the office and didn't answer him. His comments were, "How are you today? Your sounds are upsetting to your parents." I knew that if I said anything they would put me in Dayton State Mental Hospital, and I'd never get out.

I met some bizarre people during that stay. One girl came up to me and said, "You're cute. Have you ever been fucked?" My reply was, "I don't think so." Someone was always trying to get me to smoke. After two weeks of more blood tests and observation, I was dismissed with no change in my condition.

Because Dad's business kept him away from home so much, Mom decided that he needed to be home with us more. One day she and a friend stole the keys to the station, locked the doors, and declared that Dad was to find another job that would be less time consuming. I suppose Dad realized she was right, so he sold all his tools and found another job. He worked in several different places before he began working for the town, and then stayed at that job until he retired.

Chapter V

The following February I was reluctantly admitted to the psychiatric ward of University Hospital. My obsessive compulsions were really getting the best of me, as I constantly worried that Mom would die while I was gone. I'd heard of the Newman center, a church for Catholic students, and decided to get some solace by visiting the center. On the way, I remember repeatedly genuflecting in the deep snow willing those obsessions to leave.

Because I wasn't sure where the center was, I asked a young man if he could direct me to it. He offered me a ride, and of course I accepted, not thinking that this was a city and I knew nothing about him. After we drove to our destination without incident, I politely thanked him and walked into the center. I was pleasantly greeted with the sound of guitar music accompanying the Mass and a very active participation from the student congregation. There was clapping, singing, and a general feeling of friendship.

When I got back to the hospital, I relayed my invigorating experience to the staff. They were thoroughly upset with me for accepting a ride with a stranger, and took away my campus privileges for one week. They also called my parents and informed them of my caper.

Two weeks after my privileges were reinstated, I again went to the Newman Center. This time I sat behind two very pretty girls, and after Mass we started chatting about how great the guitars sounded. I learned that their last name was Campbell, and immediately began singing the Campbell soup commercial. My rendition must not have been too bad, as they asked if I wanted a ride to the campus.

Since it was very cold, I completely forgot about my last escapade and accepted. Because I wasn't about to tell them that I was a patient in the hospital psych. ward, I told them that my mother was in the hospital and was dying from cancer. All the way from church we sang songs from the guitar Mass, and they cordially took me to the front door of the hospital. I thanked them and asked them to pray for my mom.

Like a complete idiot I again told the staff at the hospital what had transpired. Once more I lost my privileges and my parents were notified.

This two- week hospital stay was a very disturbing one. Many of the patients were receiving electric shock therapy along with strong sedatives that caused them to walk around the wards like zombies, and it was very frightening to observe them. During that stay I again had numerous blood tests, x-rays, and as usual, was observed by every white-coated person in the hospital. We were not informed of any diagnosis at the time, but I was eventually sent home on a low dose of the medication Haloperidol, or Haldol.

After returning home and taking the medication, I became very lethargic. At times my legs would hardly function, making it difficult to walk to school. It was also a chore to get up in the morning, and Mom or Dad would have to pull me from my bed. Because of my lethargy and obsessive compulsions, I missed fifty-six days of school that first semester. I was still obsessed with thinking that my mom was dying or was dead, so I either frequently went home to check on her, or played sick and didn't go to school at all. When I did attend school, I called home at every opportunity to see how she was.

The following month my parents made the decision to have me admitted to Upham Hall at University Hospital for long term therapy. I was determined not to go back to that place, and ran from Dad for about two hours until he caught me. Finally we were all on our way back to Columbus, but not before I made one last try for freedom. I grabbed the steering wheel and ran the car into a tree stump. Dad's patience had reached its limit, and he gave me the whipping of my life! I spent the rest of the trip in the back seat of the car crying myself to sleep.

Because my symptoms were considered to be psychological, I was admitted to the adult psychiatric ward at Upham Hall. Mom was warned that if I didn't cooperate I would be transferred upstairs to the adolescent unit. That unit consisted of teenagers with every conceivable problem. Many were drug addicts and runaways who had experienced more in their short lives than most people would in a lifetime. On the adult floor, the other patients kept to themselves most of the time.

It took only two to three weeks for me to get transferred upstairs. I was still unresponsive in group therapy, and still exhibited loud tics. I was given a room with three other boys. It soon became evident that we were not at all compatible, and my parents were astonished at the profanity I was exposed to. This was unrelated to the coprolalia associate with Tourette Syndrome. I soon found that it was an ordinary occurrence to go into the restroom and find someone cutting his wrist with a razor blade until it bled profusely.

Demerits were issued for misbehavior, and I accumilated a record fifty-two demerits the first week. When asked why I had so many, they said, "Because you are a manipulator." My next question was, "What's a manipulator?" They answered by giving me another demerit.

Sometime during those first months, Neil Armstrong was visiting his home town in Wapakoneta, Ohio, and I desperately wanted to see him. After much pleading with my psychiatrist, he promised that if I could run around the track at the Ohio State stadium in less than a minute, he would grant me a leave. They were reluctant to let me go home because they thought my parents were largely responsible for my problems.

My psychiatrist was no dummy and he knew I could never succeed in that endeavor. I knew it too, but thought that if I would just happen to fall into a pothole on the track and become slightly injured, he would feel sorry for me and let me go home to recuperate. Sad to say, this plan didn't work. My ankle was only sprained, so I had to resort to a different tactic. Later in the year after I worked hard enough to run the track in the required time, I got to go home.

The doctors and nurses were always thinking of ways to boost morale, and as part of our treatment, planned various activities for us. One of the most memorable outings was a camping trip to some place in Vinton County, the poorest area in the state of Ohio, located about two hours from Columbus. Just before we left on our trip, I received word of the death of my maternal grandmother. She had been ill for most of her married life, and after numerous consultations and hospitalizations, no diagnosis was made. In spite of her problems she always found the time and energy to do special things for people.

Before he met Grandma, Grandpa settled in Maria Stein and became friends with the Oppenheim family who had started a small factory to make farm machinery. After several years, when the factory grew too large for its present location, they moved it to Coldwater and named it the "New Idea." Grandpa moved to Coldwater where he was hired to keep the boilers running in that factory.

Soon my grandma, who had graduated from business school, was hired to work in the accounting department. According to the older members of the Hausfeld family, the two of them met when Grandpa, who emptied the trash at the end of the day, passed her and she showed him her pretty petticoat. After they married, they bought a large house in Coldwater and raised a family of five boys and two girls.

Grandpa was very fortunate to always have a job during the depression, so Grandma baked countless pies and helped provide food for families who had no income. Some of my fondest memories are of the yearly Hausfeld reunions. They were started in Maria Stein, Ohio, and later held at the Coldwater park in one of the shelter houses. The reunions were always held on Father's Day, and it was great to meet all the relatives, especially those that came from long distances. We always played games to help everyone get acquainted. After 80 years they were discontinued because the majority of the families moved to distant places making it too difficult to return each year. I relentlessly begged to go home for Grandma's funeral, but was refused permission. My psychiatrist felt that my problems were the result of the way my parents raised me, and did not want me to return to those surroundings.

So after the kitchen help prepared our food, we embarked for a week of camping. One evening another patient, whom I'll call Gus, became tired of camping and bonding with his shrink. He grabbed the wood-cutting ax and chased his doctor intending to sever his head. I remember crawling under the blankets and praying to St. Joseph for a happy death. Gus was finally subdued and admitted to the Athens State Hospital where he stayed until we all returned to Columbus.

The usual form of recreation re-emerged during this excursion, particularly at night, and because I was a light sleeper I overheard quite a bit of this activity. One night I heard a chaperone whisper to one of the girls, "If you behave, I'll let you touch it, but don't grab too hard." I doubted that this incident was part of the poor girl's sex education, but decided to ignore the episode and return to sleep. On the day of the funeral, our leaders ordered us to put the canoes on the water at Nelsonville, and paddle our way down the Hocking River to Athens. We were to dock our canoes and sleep on the Ohio University's golf course. It was a beautiful day, but my thoughts were on Grandma's burial rather than on our trip.

About mid-afternoon, the current began to get rocky, and our boat overturned. Amid the screams of terror and swearing, the members of one of the four canoes began a rebellion by hurling sandwiches, cans of pop, cartons of milk, and expletives at one another. When things finally got under control, nothing was left to eat.

At ten o'clock that night we had not yet reached our place of rest. I was paddling one of the canoes, becoming more tired and hungry with every stroke, and finally exclaimed, "I quit!" In unison, everyone else stopped, and we all docked our canoes. With our wet shoes and clothes, our walk seemed endless until we finally arrived at a gas station. To add to the confusion, one of the patients felt that she needed a prophylactic injection for the seizure that she felt she was going to have. Imagine ten to fifteen psych patients trying to safely cross a busy highway in that situation.

The gas station was about to close, and Mr. Sparn, one of our chaperones, asked if he could make a call to the police. The manager had no idea who we were or where we came from, but allowed us to use his phone. In fifteen minutes The Athens' Police and Sheriff's Departments were at the station.

When Mr. Sparn explained to the hospital staff that one of the patients needed an injection for seizures, and that we were from a mental ward, no one got too close to us. I overheard one nurse ask another, "What is this world coming to?" I could see her point. We were all filthy and irritable. Our fellow patient received her injection, and the police took us to a vacant dorm room on Ohio U's campus to sleep. After a nearly sleepless night, we were returned to camp. We arrived back at Upham Hall the end of the week and

I doubt that anyone ever again suggested a camp-out. Two weeks later my first cousin was killed in an auto accident, and again I was refused a leave to attend the funeral.

Being in the hospital didn't free us from attending school, as it was held for one-half of the year on the ward. Our teacher seemed to be a hippie, and did not appreciate my tics. One day he said, "Frank, if you make one more fucking sound, you're going to special care." Despite an extreme effort, I was unable to control myself and was escorted to that dreadful place.

To get to "special care" you had to go through a locked wooden door and down a hallway where there were four cells. Security cell 3 was behind a steel door, and its contents were a pad and a pillow. I spent that night on the floor with no contact with anyone except an occasional check by a guard.

Another night I was in bed, disturbing everyone else with my tics, when one of the orderlies grabbed me under the arms and dragged me to the cell. He paraded me in front of all the other patients who were screaming, laughing, and hissing at me.

I was in "special care" about six times while in Upham Hall. and developed severe claustrophobia from the experience. Elevators give me a sick feeling, so I use the stairway whenever possible.

There were other occurrences to make that place so frightening. One day one of the female patients confiscated a huge needle and syringe and stuck the needle into my leg. We were behind a window, and I had to scream for a nurse, who eventually came and pulled the needle out. Her only reaction was, "Oh, she didn't mean anything by it. She was just fooling around."

We also had to report to the swimming pool for exercise every week. Our leader was a huge man who seemed to dislike me immediately. In every session he held my head under the water until my lungs nearly burst. I was unable to fight him, and there were no witnesses besides other patients to come to my defense.

Of course, our knife wielding fellow patient was still among us. He was a tall, thin young man who wore beads, had long hair, and smoked pot at every available opportunity. I never learned his diagnosis, but he had a girl friend and was convinced that I was out to steal her from him. On one occasion he pushed me to the floor and tried to choke me. It took several attendants to restrain him and free me.

After about a year of confinement with no signs of improvement, all of my privileges were revoked. I was no longer allowed walks outside, no extra visitors, and worst of all, no visits from my mom because she was considered to be the cause of my problems by being overly protective of me. Until then, Dad and Mom had been to see me at least once a week, and this punishment was to last six to eight weeks. Following a month of this isolation, Dad arrived unannounced one day, and we escaped down a back door to meet Mom who was waiting in the car. I'll never forget her pounding her head on the dash board, crying about what a terrible mother she was. We visited for a half-hour, and then I had to return, only to be issued more demerits.

My doctor was a born-again Christian, and I spent several nights at his home. He tried to convince me that if I said the "sinners' prayer," I would be forgiven and be healed. I told him that I would be glad to join his religion if it would cure me. I was desperate to get well, and would have done anything to be normal. After attending his service, he accepted my invitation to participate in Mass at the Newman Center with the understanding that he would not receive Holy Communion. To my dismay, he followed me to the front of church and received communion. I was sure that my fate was doomed. To me it was unthinkable for a Protestant to receive the host in the Catholic Church!

On May 28, 1970, after I had been there for 18 months, my parents were told that I was a hopeless case and should be committed to a psychiatric hospital for the rest of my life. Mom did not mince any words telling them where to go, and we went home.

The drive home was a fiasco. My tics were so violent that they shook the car and Dad was slowly losing his patience. Just as he was ready to turn around and slap me, Mom said, "For God's sake, leave him alone, Jim. He's been through two years of hell and has only gotten worse ! I love you, Frank, and I know that you can't help what's happening to you." Dad then apologized for his behavior, and we completed the long journey home.

I would be remiss if I did not acknowledge the fact that I received many cards, letters, etc. during my hospitalization. Tonya Giere took care of my sister whenever Dad and Mom came to visit me, and she wrote every week without fail. Those letters were certainly a welcome sight in a place that seemed like a hell on earth.

Chapter VI

During the summer of 1970 I felt a desperate need to make friends. Since the local swimming pool was a favorite meeting place, I became an avid lover of the water. Perhaps this was because while swimming, I was neither possessed by the incessant jerking of my body nor any of the other tics that plagued me. The vocalizations, picking at things, and eye-blinking all disappeared, and life almost seemed normal. Yet after being in the hospital for two years, I did not feel as if I really had any friends my age and remained the brunt of much mockery. But it was good to be home and I wanted to stay there.

My parents thought I needed a break from all the harassment, and two weeks before the start of my junior year, they flew me to California to visit my grandma who was staying with my Aunt Joan. I spent the evening before the flight in the park at a softball tournament. While talking with Pat and Pam (two of the girls who had befriended me), I remarked that I needed to get to know some guys to hang around with, but they all seemed to mock me because of my tics. They suggested that I approach Dave, George, and Randy, who were at the ball game. Mustering all the courage I could get, I approached the three of them, and began a conversation. At one point when I felt they were making fun of me, I said, "Hey, I've had enough of that. Give me some slack. I don't have a friend in the world. I just got out of the nut house and could certainly use some companionship." Things changed after that, and when it was time to leave, Dave offered to drive us all home. He dropped me off last, and during our conversation, assured me that when I returned, I could count on them to be friends, and could come to them with any problems. They were true to their word, and our friendship still continues.

The flight to California was without problems, and visiting there was quite an experience. It was great walking along Sunset Boulevard and Hollywood and Vine, places I'd only read about or seen in the movies. My aunt had a swimming pool, and I had a very relaxing time.

One night my tics became quite severe, so I closed all the windows. Grandma lost patience with me and chased me around the house with a broom. She threatened to call the LAPD if I didn't stop that yapping. Finally I became exhausted and fell asleep. Following that night, they all wanted to admit me to the UCLA psychiatric ward, and when I insisted that I wanted to go home, they would not let me. They felt that I should be admitted to a hospital in California for further evaluation. I finally called my parents and told them that I definitely wanted to come home. I had some friends now and wanted to graduate from Coldwater High School. Reluctantly they acceded to my plan, and I flew home.

Mom was against my returning to school because of the trouble I had in the past, but the day after arriving home, I met with Mr. Pax, the principal, and we worked out a schedule. Two weeks later I was back in school.

I would like to say that everything went well, but a typical class I attended was filled with, "Well! Well! Well! Well!"—constant repetitions with increasing volume, and "Arp! Arp! Arp!" (sounds like barking). At the same time my arms and legs would jerk violently, causing havoc in the room. We had an assistant priest at that time whose name was Father Reidel. For some reason, out of nowhere, I would blurt out, "Fu-fu-fu-fu-fu-fu-Father Reidel!" One teacher thought I was swearing and nearly kicked me out of class. My friends still claim that when a teacher I didn't like passed my desk, my leg would involuntarily jerk out in front of him, as if I were trying to trip him. Mr. Pax tried so hard to make things work, but my tics constantly disrupted every class, and in the end, I more or less studied on my own.

My social life was almost non-existent, and when I did get out, I usually embarrassed everyone by shouting such things as, "She's-she's-sh-sh-she's so cute-cute-cute!" whenever we encountered a pretty girl. Most of my friends went to the football games, either as fans or to participate in the band. It was so much fun for everyone, but that was ruined for me by some of the fans in the cheering section who held up signs saying, "FRANK SAYS GO ARF ARF TEAM!" It became easier to stay home than to tolerate such ridicule.

In spite of everything going wrong, I did have some good times in school that fall, as I actually joined the cross country team and experienced the thrill of running five miles through the park and surrounding areas. I would never have completed the first race if it hadn't ended on the track around the football field where the team was practicing. I was in second-to-last place because one guy fell into the creek and another one fainted. I was about to stop running because of exhaustion when my friends on the team shouted the encouragement I needed to finish the race.

One of our meets was in the small town of Mendon where the course was run around corn and bean fields. After a while they all looked alike but someone was supposed to be at the halfway mark to steer us in the right direction. I ran and ran with no sight of our lookout before I finally spotted some students in the distance. One of them was the girl who was designated to be our guide. Evidently the race had been over for some time, and I had become completely lost.

I never did become proficient at running, but the enjoyment of being on the team was priceless. Running in the country with the fresh air that many times contained the aroma of newly spread manure, was something that I'll never forget. I'll also never forget what a classmate of mine did to me in the locker room one day. After we showered, he took me aside, explaining that all that running would cause me to get very sore in the "private area," and gave me some cream to rub there to "prevent the soreness." Of course the cream was one used by athletes for muscle soreness, and after I applied it, I was doing a wild dance. I hurried home, undressed, and showered until I got some relief from the heat. The rest of the seniors knew what a jerk their classmate was, so after they heard about the episode, they hung around and provided protection for me whenever I had to shower.

I also joined the drama club that year when they put on a production of "The Lark," a play about Saint Joan of Arc. Pam Noll, my cousin, convinced Greg Myers, the director, to let me audition, and I was given the role of the Archbishop of Reims, France. This lofty endeavor included practices nightly for several months. Performances were held on Saturday and Sunday nights, each lasting two-and-a-half hours. After I completed both without exhibiting one tic, everyone was prompted to say, "There's nothing wrong with you. It's all a big act!" This criticism eventually spread to the general public, and many of them were saying, "That kid is not sick. He spent both nights on the stage without making any funny noises. He just does that for attention!" Actually, when I was given a part in the play, the director warned me that if I exhibited one unnecessary noise, my part would be given to someone else. It was also another example of how my tics could be controlled for a time with severe concentration

After the final production we were all invited to a party given by one of the parents. I attended for a while, then excused myself and went outside. The air was brisk from an early snow that night, but I walked to my friend Pat's house. Pat was dating Dave at that time, and I coaxed her into driving around with the hope of meeting Dave and the guys. We found Dave and George, and Pat invited them to her house. What a great experience that was! We were there for several hours, and I felt truly accepted by all of them. Even though my tics were in full swing, it didn't bother them, so it didn't bother me.

Dave and George had girl friends who took much of their time, but they also knew how lonely I was and made every effort to include me in their plans whenever they didn't have dates. Disco was in its prime at that time, and we would hang out at the S & S bar where they played all the latest tunes. I did try to dance with some of the girls, but soon found that I was too much of a klutz to impress them, and spent most of the time dancing alone among strangers. I dressed exactly like John Trivolta in jeans, silk shirt, pleated jean jacket, and high topped shoes. No one mocked me because the music was so loud that they probably did not hear any of my tics, and most of them had enough to drink that it wouldn't have bothered them anyway.

Although my tics were very bad, I was glad that God had blessed me with good friends who accepted me for what I was. They teased me at times, but I felt so at ease with them that I reciprocated in kind. To this day I am amazed that they took me under their wings without knowing that I actually had an illness that was causing all of my crazy actions.

John Gast, one of the guys in our crowd whose parents went to Florida in the winter, always had at least one good party while they were gone. At one of them, Dave met Jill who eventually took Pat's place in his life. It was a very difficult time for Pat, and since I liked her very much, it was also difficult for me. We all learned that life is full of changing events, and most of them change for a good reason.

By the end of December my tics were out of control, and since Grandma was still in California, I moved back into her trailer which was located several blocks from our house. Dad stayed with me during the night about a month, and after that I stayed alone for a year and a half. As soon as it became known that I was alone, the abuse started—loud knocks on the door with mocking tic noises.

School was becoming more difficult, as I seemed to lose the ability to concentrate for any amount of time. I took copious notes in every class, but had no recollection of writing them. These symptoms are a result of ADHD, or attention deficit hyperactivity disorder, the inability to concentrate and retain information that is received. It is another common segment of Tourette Syndrome. Naturally my grades dropped, and since my only close friends graduated that year, I felt lost.

One evening while riding my bike around town, I noticed some familiar boys playing basketball on a backyard court, so I stopped to watch. A man and his wife were observing the game from their steps, and we began conversing. I learned that their last name was Kanney, and that Vince had been a classmate of my Aunt Joan. When he asked me how she was, I replied, "They're all nuts in California." Everyone laughed, and I remember thinking how great it was that no one was making fun of me. That was the start of a lasting friendship, and their home became my place of refuge. When someone told me that Marilyn was a registered nurse, my first thought was, "Maybe she can figure out what's wrong with me."

Gradually I began hanging out at the Kanney household. They had six children who got along as well as most siblings, and were always teasing each other. On one occasion the youngest daughter, Lisa, offered me a peanut butter and jelly sandwich, but instead of jelly, she substituted catsup. I chased her around the house, and actually felt as if I had a family who accepted me for what I was, and not for something they wanted me to be.

Our town has a beautiful park that was the scene of ball games and other social events. One evening I struck up a conversation with some local farm boys who were visiting in town. Things were going fine until they threatened to put a cattle- probe up my rectum. If you've ever seen a cattle- probe, you can imagine my fear. I fled that park faster than the speed of light, and somehow evaded them by hiding behind bushes and taking all the back streets to the Kanneys where I stayed until it was safe to go home.

Marilyn worked with my mother, and one evening told her that she felt I could be treated with the proper diagnosis. Mom agreed not to institutionalize me, and promised to do everything she could to facilitate my recovery. She kept that promise, and nearly moved heaven and earth to do so.

I graduated that spring in spite of the fact that my grades averaged D and D minuses. Until the seventh grade, my lowest grade was B minus. I honestly think that they were all glad to get me out of the school system. After the graduation ceremony, the super-intendent of schools and one of my former teachers met with Dad and offered their assistance in dealing with me. Whenever I think of some of the teachers who tried to help me, I also think of some who made fun of me. One teacher would hear me coming down the hallway, and say to the other students, "All right everybody! Guess who is coming down the hall! Everyone, listen! I'll give you two guesses." It always caused an embarrassing moment for me when I finally made it to the classroom.

Several days after graduation our baseball team went to the state finals in Columbus. I went along to the game with Marilyn and some of the Kanney clan. She did not know the precise directions to the playing field, so I was to be the navigator since I was "familiar" with Columbus. We still laugh about that trip for many reasons. Her children and my ridiculous tics were bad enough, but her navigator recommended a wrong turn, heading us into downtown Columbus. Somehow we managed to get to the baseball field in time, and had much fun even though we lost the ball game.

Our town holds a yearly Community Picnic where everyone congregates and spends money to benefit the park and library. That summer during the picnic I was walking through the park at about 10:30 P.M. when I met an old acquaintance who was known to use drugs at times. He was accompanied by a fellow user I'll call Bo, who was obviously coming down from a drug high. Bo was a well- built guy, a former football player or wrestler, whom one wouldn't want to cross. However, when he offered me some of his "medication," I couldn't resist giving him a lecture about how God doesn't want us to use drugs.

Eventually a former classmate of mine and another friend arrived in a jeep pulling a hay wagon. They both got out of the jeep and walked toward us. Suddenly they grabbed me by the neck, put me into the wagon and exclaimed, "We're going to take you out to Buschur Road, blindfold you, take off your clothes to see if you're a man, and make you walk home!" I let out the loudest scream I could manage, and with that, Bo ran to the wagon, grabbed my ex-classmate, and shouted, "You're nothing but a fucking S.O.B.! Get Frank out of that wagon now, or you're going to pay for it. I'm coming down off drugs, and really don't care what I do to you. I want you to know that Frank has my phone number, and if I hear that you've touched one hair on his head, I'll beat you to death!"

I got out of there promptly, and I'm sure the instigators did the same. I was afraid to go back to the trailer, and not finding the Kanneys at home, crept around town for hours until I felt the danger was over.

My mother was determined to learn my final diagnosis from my stay at Upham Hall, and in 1972 she finally persuaded Dr. Beare to get my records released from the hospital. When the records arrived, my final diagnosis was listed as "Gilles de la Tourette Syndrome," Several months later Dr. Beare attended a seminar in New York City where they discussed the little known disease known as Tourette Syndrome. Apparently a doctor by the name of Dr. Shapiro was doing much research into this disease, and having some success with its treatment. After returning home, Dr. Beare discussed his findings with my mom who immediately agreed that I should certainly be evaluated by this physician.

In 1973 after a long wait, my parents received a letter from Dr. Shapiro informing them that he wanted me to be admitted to New York Hospital, associated with Cornell University. Now there was no way I was going to New York City and be confined to another hospital, so I intercepted all the correspondence from Dr Shapiro and hid it. This was quite easy, as both my parents worked, and I came home at noon and brought in the mail.

Finally on the seventh of February, the doctor phoned my mom, and I knew that I was in trouble. Arrangements were promptly made for my admission to the hospital, and we began to prepare for it. I first called my cousin Pam who was in nursing school. She reassured me that we were taking the right steps. We discussed what type of hospital it was, and she said that they probably did abortions there. I feared that since they had no respect for life, I probably would not make it out alive. Nevertheless, arrangements were made for my sister to stay with my aunt and uncle, and we flew to New York City.

Chapter VII

After an uneventful flight and landing, we took a cab and drove for 45 minutes to the hospital, located in the middle of Manhattan. We had no idea what this hospital was like, and for some reason, did not expect what we encountered. What a delight it was to find it very impressive in a beautiful setting. A light coating of snow covered the ground, and the first thing we noticed on approaching from the oval drive was the sign on the entrance of the building. It read, "New York Hospital," and beneath a picture depicting the Good Samaritan was the caption, "Go and do thou likewise." Little did I know how much they would become good Samaritans to me during my stay at that institution.

We were met by the doctor's secretary who directed us to a waiting area. Security guards surrounded the place, so we all felt very safe in spite of being in such a huge city. It was a two-hour wait for the doctor's arrival, and as usual my tics were frozen by fear. I was silent the entire time.

Finally we were greeted by Dr. Shapiro, who appeared to be a rather large, tall man with thinning white hair, who reminded me of my grandfather. (I recently learned that I was completely mistaken about his stature, as he was actually rather short.) His voice was quiet, but when he spoke, he commanded everyone's attention and made us all feel at ease. After he introduced himself as a psychiatrist, my first words to him were, "Oh, no! I've had enough of you SOBs!" He then pointed his finger at me and said, "It's a wonder to me and a credit to you that you haven't committed suicide. If you stay here, I'll try to prove that Tourette Syndrome is neurological and only has psychiatric complications." He then asked, "Do you like meat?" When I answered in the affirmative, he quipped, "That's good, because you're going to be eating a hell of a lot of it." It was explained to us that there was much research being done into the role of specific diets and their effect on neurological disorders. He then discussed my symptoms with Dad, who was overcome with embarrassment when told that he also exhibited tics in the form of eye blinking.

I was informed that my stay would be from six to eight weeks or several months accompanied by the advice, "You got yourself here. Now pull yourself up by your boot straps."

We eventually learned that Dr. Shapiro's first encounter with Tourette Syndrome began with a visit to a book store. While browsing, he encountered a pretty, well-dressed young woman who repeatedly uttered the words, "Fuck! Fuck! Fuck!" He became intensely interested as to what would prompt such behavior and knew there had to be some pathology that caused it. This began his research into a disease that has affected many people.

My first night was spent in a private room that overlooked a posh neighborhood with a view of the Empire State Building and the lights of Manhattan. I got out my rosary and began praying. When one of the nurses checked on me she remarked, "You're frightened, aren't you?" She reassured me until I relaxed and fell asleep.

The next day I was placed in a room with four beds, two of which were occupied. One of my roommates was Mr. Hunt, a retiree who was undergoing experimental treatment for cancer. My parents stayed in New York for one week, and with the aid of Mr. and Mrs. Hunt, toured the city by cab. It was a very emotional scene when Dad and Mom departed for home. Mom didn't want to leave, and nearly jumped out of the cab. The normally callous cab driver stopped the cab for one last good-bye.

Mrs. Hunt promised Mom that she would look after me, and she did. I was never without paper, stamps, or pens, and she was always there when I needed her.

The department where I was confined was an experimental-neurological one. My neurologist, Dr. Sweet, a man of few words, made me feel that I was going to get well and could stay as long as necessary. I told him that I was willing to stay until it could be proven that I wasn't crazy or possessed by the devil.

The first week was spent undergoing a barrage of tests: EEGs, EKGs, endless surveys, paper work, blood work, etc. My diet was scrupulously monitored to see the effect it had on my behavior. I received large amounts of protein, particularly meats, with hamburger every day for lunch and steak every evening for dinner. Apparently the diet showed no bearing on my disease, and later I was not placed on any restrictions.

Oddly, during the first weeks in the hospital, my tics had vanished. No hissing, barking, twitching, obscenities, lip biting or other annoying actions were manifested--absolutely nothing! This led the physicians to doubt my diagnosis, and in a phone interview with my parents, they expressed their concern about it. Mom must have been totally exasperated by then because when I talked to her on the phone, she said, "Start having tics or I'm flying out there to beat them out of you!" She must have shocked me back to reality as the obtrusive tics returned, and my diagnosis was confirmed.

On the beginning of the third week, Dr. Sweet told me that I was to have a spinal tap in the morning. I told Father Madigan, the chaplain who visited daily that I didn't think I would live through the procedure. The next day when they approached me with a foot-long needle (At least it looked that long!), I called for the priest. There was no way they could get that needle into my spine! It took three hefty nurses and two male orderlies to hold me down, and I underwent two taps in an eight- hour- span.

My birthday occurred about that time so the nurses threw a party for me. Later I called Susan Oberholzer, a family friend who lived in New York City. She came for me the next weekend and exclaimed, "Let's get the hell out of here!" We went to the top of the Empire State Building, and spent an unforgettable day. I was granted four hours leave every Saturday and Sunday, so Susan visited nearly every weekend and acquainted me with the city. Most of the time we went by foot and covered quite a bit of territory. A trip that I'm sure she'll never forget was to the Metropolitan Museum of Art. My tics were in full swing, and one of the most prominent of these was having to touch anyone or anything near me. The look on her face was priceless when I inadvertently touched one of the statues. Immediately the curator was on the spot, chastising me and embarrassing Susan.

I soon gained another roommate by the name of Orrin, who was about fifteen or sixteen years old. He was accompanied by his mother, and had long dark hair, wore bell-bottoms, and exhibited very loud tics. Without realizing that his actions were very similar to mine, I was repulsed by him. Many of his tics were in the form of karate movements, and very frightening when he tried to use them on me. He also brought a guitar, and played and sang for relaxation, showing no symptoms during that time. Orrin was Jewish, and when he learned about my German heritage, became very apprehensive of me. We eventually became very good friends who fully understood what Tourette Syndrome was all about. After his dismissal from the hospital he chose not to take medication because of its side effects, and became a neuro-psychiatrist. He manages to control his tics up to a point, and then has to resort to isolating himself to relieve all the demons that were suppressed. Over the ensuing years, he developed severe back problems because of all the jerky tics and spasms, and began to try various medications to combat his symptoms. Orrin is married with two children, a boy and a girl.

One of my favorite nurses, Kathy, was a tall, sexy blonde, and I, along with everyone else was infatuated with her. She always took time to talk to us, and seemed to say the right things at the right time. One day when Orrin's tics were unusually loud, I said to him, "Orrin, you're going to ruin your lungs with those loud noises." Kathy overheard this and remarked, "Frank, your smoking is not helping your lungs either."

Eventually I began meeting more of the patients who were confined, and when someone new arrived, everyone soon grew to know each other. About three months after my admission I met Ann Duerr. She was undergoing treatment for lung problems and more or less adopted me. She worked at Rockefeller Center, and on weekends, volunteered at the Sloan Kettering

Center for Cancer. Every one to two weeks when in the area, she brought me papers, pens, and other supplies. She always commented on my sense of humor in coping with Tourette Syndrome. Later, when she moved to Atlanta, she called me at home once a week for a long time. She had met Dad when he visited New York for a Tourette meeting, and during one phone conversation, learned that he was apprehensive about starting a new job. The night before his job began, she called and sang a lullaby to him. My sister and I always got cards from her with $5.00 enclosed.

My first venture into the city was a memorable experience. I was in the process of collecting a 24-hour urine specimen, so I took the urinal with me, and carried it in a paper bag. My destination was the UN building, and I planned to walk, even though it was on the opposite end of the city from the hospital, a distance of about five miles. It seemed to take forever, but I finally arrived at the prodigious institution to be greeted by the guard who wanted to check my bag. After showing him its contents, and explaining why I needed it, he was very understanding, and allowed me to keep it.

During the tour, for some reason, my kidneys went into overdrive and I overflowed the urinal, losing part of my specimen. I was sure to be in trouble when they learned of this at the hospital, so I neglected to tell them. No one ever complained about not having a sufficient quantity to run the test, so I considered myself very lucky.

In March, Susan called to announce that we were going to participate in the St. Patrick's Day parade, and although neither of us claim any Irish ancestry, we enjoyed every minute of it. By the end of the parade, we were both cold and tired, and found shelter in an Irish pub. Susan ordered Irish Coffee, so I did likewise, thinking hot coffee would be just what I needed. After a couple sips, I became very dizzy, and felt ill. I said, "Susan, we have to get back to the hospital. I feel terrible!" She quickly got me outside into the fresh air where I proceeded to hang onto a light post to keep from falling off the earth. "Why-why-y-y-y did you let me drink that, S-S-S-Susan?" I asked. She replied, "Well, you're old enough, and I thought you knew what Irish coffee was."

We both felt that a good brisk walk would cure me, so I suggested that we go to the St. Patrick's Cathedral. Susan was totally against this, as she had not gone to church in years. After much coercion, I talked her into going there. We arrived in time for Mass, and I could feel her discomfort through the entire hour. I was still carrying my balloon from the parade, and somehow it got loose, floating among the Cardinals' hats that were hanging from the ceiling. What a fitting ending to a St. Patrick's Day parade!

I don't know how I would have made it through my hospitalization if it hadn't been for Susan. Besides taking me to all the interesting places, she would remain afterwards and help me get settled. Sometimes when the pains in my legs became unbearable, she would rub them until the pain subsided, and I could relax and sleep. I'll never forget all the thoughtful things she did for me and will always consider her one of my greatest benefactors.

Chapter VIII

Throughout my hospitalization, I received the Daily Standard, a newspaper from Celina, and the Chronicle, a weekly newspaper from Coldwater. Chunkol, a tiny Asian nurse from Thailand, thoroughly enjoyed reading the newspapers from home. She loved the descriptions of weddings with the pictures, and swore that when she died, she wanted her obituary to appear only in those papers. She was especially curious about the number of problems we encountered from drinking, and wondered if that was the prime method of entertainment in our area.

There were no laundry facilities at the hospital, so my clothes were getting pretty rank. Our head nurse, Linda must have gotten wind of this dilemma, and told me to either get my clothes laundered or go home. She was from Youngstown, Ohio, had a very professional manner, and always wore her nurse's cap. I managed to wash my underwear in the bathroom sink, and by chance, while on one of my walks, met a lady who directed me to a Chinese laundry. The proprietor spoke no English, so we conversed in a type of sign language. It wasn't easy getting her to understand that I wanted no starch in my underwear, as my tics made this type of communication nearly impossible.

I was still undergoing various medical tests such as head CT scans and blood work, and was placed on some experimental medications. No one ever said what the medicines were, but none of them seemed to be effective. My diet was constantly evaluated, and besides being high in protein, contained plenty of vegetables and fruit In addition to the food, I had to drink 40 ounces of distilled water a day.

During one of my trips around the city, I discovered the St. Catherine of Sienna Church. It possessed a huge statue of St. Jude, the patron saint of hopeless cases. The hospital grounds were filled with beautiful fresh flowers, so I took the liberty of picking a few nearly every Saturday and placing them before the statue, praying for an end to my illness. After a while my conscience got the better of me, and I confessed this bit of thievery to Father Madigan. He laughed and said, "With so many flowers available here, it's good that a few of them are being used for a good cause."

The idea of placing flowers before a statue was strange to everyone there, so when I decided to seek permission to make a May altar in honor of the Blessed Virgin, I was asked by one of the nurses, "What the hell is a May altar?" After explaining its purpose and receiving the go- ahead, I went scouting for flowers. The best buy I could make was for two lilacs for the ridiculous price of $7.50. I told everyone, "Where I come from, lilacs are given away." Nevertheless, I bought them, and after placing them in a vase with water, put them before a small plastic statue of Mary on the radiator in my room. That night the weather turned cold, so of course they turned on the heat. You can imagine my chagrin when the next morning, I found my $7.50 lilacs wilted beyond recognition!

That week another memorable patient was admitted. Her name was Kathy Marshall, and she was from Stamford, Connecticut. She was being treated for adrenal insufficiency and hormonal growth problems. After our dismissal from the hospital, we continued our correspondence, and in one of her letters she wrote, "Life is a series of losses—parents, relatives, friends, and eventually yourself." Kathy certainly had her share of disappointments, but she was always there to offer support to others. She eventually became one of those sad but not forgotten losses when she passed away from her illness.

Shortly before Easter, while conversing with Father Madigan, I mentioned that I had played the organ in church at home. Since Father was in need of an organist for the hospital's chapel, I began to play for Masses every Sunday. There was no music available, so I had to improvise all the hymns.

I spent the three hours of Good Friday praying in bed. I was so well indoctrinated into following the rituals of Holy Week that it just seemed to be the right thing to do. Orrin could not understand why I was so quiet. That evening, Dorothy, another patient on our floor, became hungry for a big blueberry muffin from the deli. Dorothy was a tall, pretty, blonde, blue-eyed immigrant who spoke with a noticeable German accent. Things were rather calm that evening, so I talked her into slipping away for about an hour to the deli on 1st Avenue. She purchased a large mouth-watering buttered blueberry muffin, and what a temptation that muffin was! It was a forbidden fruit on my diet, so I had to imagine how delicious it must have been. Dorothy and I remained good friends throughout her hospitalization, and before her dismissal, she presented me with a transistor radio so I could listen to music at all times.

On Holy Saturday I took Orrin to the St. Catherine of Sienna Church. He was very impressed with the twenty Dominican Fathers chanting their daily prayers, but he could not figure out why we prayed for the Jews. In turn, he promised to take me to his temple some day, but for some reason that visit never occurred.

Easter Sunday arrived, and I decided to go to Mass at Saint Patrick's Cathedral. I started walking the long distance when a cab happened to come by. Since it was unoccupied, I splurged and engaged it. The cabby was not into the Easter spirit, as evidenced by his fare, so I did not tip him.

The cathedral was awesome! There must have been two million lilacs, hyacinths, lilies—-all types of flowers! I was met by a police officer at the door who demanded my ticket. I informed him that I was a Catholic and didn't need a ticket. He answered with, "I don't care if you're Jewish. You need a ticket." After I made numerous unsuccessful attempts to sneak into the building, the Bishop permitted everyone without a ticket to approach the altar, and we all got front row seats. The entire service was beautiful beyond words, from the procession, the Mass with Cardinal Cooke presiding, to the choir and organist. I had tics throughout the Mass, and cried buckets, but fortunately all of this was drowned out by the most beautiful organ and choir I had ever heard. At the end of Mass the large gates at the entrance were opened, and we were personally introduced to the Cardinal by his secretary. He gave each of us his blessing while we knelt and kissed his ring. After Mass we marched in the Easter Parade for five miles down 5th Avenue, joining in the singing of The Easter Parade.

Shortly after Easter, I decided to attend the musical "Godspell" and had a terrific time. I treated myself to a Pepsi and Reese's candy bar, and became acquainted with a woman who chain-smoked, bumming cigarettes from everyone. After the production, there was a fine drizzle of rain outside, but that didn't stop an entourage of exuberant theater-goers from parading hand in hand down the sidewalk singing songs from the show. It made no difference that we were all strangers. A day or two later, I would regret the Pepsi and candy bar, as sugar crystals were found in my urine, and I was again threatened with dismissal. Another lesson was learned the hard way.

Susan Bloch was admitted about this time. She had kidney failure and was receiving dialysis. Her room was situated two doors from mine, and I'll always feel extremely fortunate to have known her. At the time of her hospitalization, she was the director of public relations for the "Repertory Theater" of Lincoln Center, and at the same time, conceived and administered a graduate course in theater at Fordham University. She was also producing "Theater Highlights" for a radio station and running a graphic arts program between the Pratt Institute and the Lincoln Center Theater. She had graduated from Syracruse University, and did graduate work there and at the Ceylon Academy of Fine Arts in Sri Lanka. These were merely a fraction of her accomplishments, and because of her various occupations, she had many friends in the entertainment business.

I remember Susan as being tall and very pretty, with long dark hair worn in a bun. She invited me to her home on numerous occasions, and these were usually gala events. She always introduced me as her friend, "Frank, who is the best thing to happen to me." In the ensuing years, when I developed the persistent tic of saying the "F" word, she would add, "If I said fuck in public, I'd get arrested, but Frank can say it to anyone and get by with it." If that statement sounds ridiculous today, you must remember that this occurred in the70s when that word was considered the ultimate in profanity. While in the hospital, Susan received roses from David Bernie, a prominent actor starring in the television series, "Bridget Loves Bernie." I doubt that you'll find reruns of that series today.

Another patient arrived about the same time. His name was Chester Bowles, and he was being treated for Parkinson's disease. During quiet times, I would slip into his room, and he would entertain me with stories about his presidential acquaintances. It was evident that he thought highly of JFK, and was a staunch Democrat.

I knew that he had been an ambassador to India, appointed by President Truman, but only recently learned that he was a prestigious American diplomat and public administrator, who held numerous high offices, including governor of Connecticut, twice ambassador to India, a member of the House of Representatives from Connecticut, and special advisor to the president on African, Asian, and Latin affairs. President Truman appointed him director of the Office of Economic Stabilization, a position from which he resigned four months later in protest against legislation diluting his authority over price control. I've also learned that he was the author of several books, and I hope to read them some day.

Early in May, I became very homesick with the arrival of spring. The windows were never opened because of air conditioning, and I went into a deep depression. I stayed in bed most of the time, ate little, and didn't shower for five days. Since I was on such a strict diet the doctors worried about the lack of calories and its effect on me. They told me that if I didn't eat, they'd have to send me home.

On Thursday of that week, my parents were informed of the situation. They were both very concerned, so Dad arranged to fly to New York on the weekend. Worried and restless, they stayed awake that night until 4: 00 o'clock when Dad decided to change his flight plans and leave in the morning. Mom was unable to accompany him because she was recovering from foot surgery. Dad rose early, went to Grandma's, and borrowed five-hundred dollars for the trip.

What a surprise it was when he arrived! We both cried and clung to one another, and in spite of the fact that our relationship had been very strained recently, we sat for a long time and discussed my problems. Dad gave me the strength to get up, shower, and continue on with life. We spent the entire weekend talking while walking around the city.

Dr. Shapiro came periodically to check on my progress, and he was often accompanied by his wife, Elaine. Dr. Shapiro was an M.D. and a Clinical Associate Professor of Psychiatry, while his wife possessed a Ph.D. with a Research Associate in Psychiatry. Elaine was strikingly beautiful, with dark black shoulder-length hair. I liked her immediately, and found it very easy to converse with her. During their visits I tried desperately to suppress my tics, but invariably they would surface.

In the spring another member of the Shapiro team arrived after finishing her psychiatric residency. Dr. Bruun had an avid interest in Tourette Syndrome and was very sympathetic with anyone suffering from the disease. We had many long conversations, and when I was dismissed from the hospital, she agreed to keep me up to date on any new developments that arose in the treatment of Tourette's. She was true to her word, and we corresponded by her sending me Christmas cards, and my sending her Hanukkah cards. One year I received her card with a note attached saying that although she really appreciated my cards, she felt I should know that she wasn't Jewish. She assumed that with the name of Bonifas, I wasn't either. I called her at her office, and we both had a good laugh. We now send each other Christmas and Easter cards.

As part of our therapy, Orrin and I needed some exercise, so were granted use of the swimming pool. Since I had no bathing suit, and very limited shopping experience, Susan Oberholzer again came to the rescue by taking me to Bloomingdales. I was completely unprepared for such a huge place, and the corresponding huge price of my suit. At one point we got separated, and I envisioned myself spending the rest of my life wandering around that immense store trying to escape.

Dr. Sweet also made frequent rounds, and always chided me about smoking. He would say, "Frank, if you insist on smoking, you're going to die from lung cancer some day." I would reply, "Oh, no. I can quit any time I want." He'd answer, "Then show me." I'd counter with, "Not now." Those words still haunt me, as I've still been unable to stop that miserable habit.

Over Memorial Day weekend, Mom flew to New York with Ann, her first cousin's daughter. We all spent the day in New Jersey at the home of another of her first cousins. As usual, the food was plentiful, delicious looking, and not on my diet. I couldn't help but suspect that eating was the favorite pastime in the area. In the evening, Mom and I took the bus back to the hospital. By that time my tics would no longer be silenced, and Mom was sure that we would be mugged or murdered. We were neither, and the bus driver dropped us safely at the student nurses' dorm where Mom stayed the night. Before walking back to the hospital, she gave me orders to call her immediately when I got to my room, but by then my medication was taking full effect, and I promptly fell asleep. Poor Mom spent half that night worrying that I had been abducted.

Several weeks later, after I had started on another experimental drug, Mom's cousins again invited me to spend the day with them. I took the train to Grand Central Station and then boarded a bus to take me near their house. While on the bus, I experienced severe tics, but after explaining to the other passengers that I had Tourette Syndrome, no questions were asked. My bus stop was in the middle of nowhere in front of a gas station, and my medication was reaching its full potential. Unfortunately, I had forgotten to bring a copy of my relatives' phone number, and could not recall what it was. Any other time I would have been frightened silly, but the medication had a calming effect, and I weathered the storm until my hosts arrived about 20 minutes later.

The first weekend in June, Susan O.'s boyfriend, Dave, a New York City cab driver, came for me at the hospital. I had never met him, and became somewhat apprehensive when faced with eight cabs waiting for their fares. "Hey Frank!" was a long-awaited and welcome sound, and since I was the only Frank waiting, this had to be my ride. We drove to Greenwich Village and Susan's apartment which consisted of two small rooms with a very steep monthly rent. Dave was off duty, so we toured New York City all day. After a sightseeing expedition that I'll always remember, we ended up in Little Italy in time for the St. Anthony Festival where great food was again abundant. I swore that when I got out of that city, I'd eat myself silly with all sorts of rich food.

That same week, I began therapy with injections of Haldol, the drug I had received at Upham Hall. They gave me large doses of the medication by injection, and it completely abolished my tics. However, I developed severe lethargy, muscle spasms, and akinesia (Parkinson-like symptoms), making it impossible to get out of bed. Because of the side effects, the dosage was gradually decreased and they added Cogentin and Darvon to combat the reactions.

In only two days the spasms were drastically reduced, and my tics were gone! For the first time in years, my body was not jumping around. I wasn't biting my lips, and there were no more loud emanations. I felt like a normal human being and shouted, "Give glory to God for this miracle drug!" Eventually the shots were changed to pills and the doctors called Dad and Mom with the news that I could be discharged. They were ecstatic, but also apprehensive, so Dad came to New York for two days to observe me.

When Father Madigan had Mass that Sunday, his homily was about me and my miraculous recovery. Everyone in the chapel was crying for joy. Father was so overcome with emotion that he had to end his sermon and continue with the Mass.

There was one more task to accomplish before going home, and that was to place flowers for the last time on the altar of St. Jude at St. Catherine's Church. This meant getting permission to leave the hospital from Linda, the head nurse. Her reaction to this request was about what I had expected, and after much coaxing from me, she threw up her arms in resignation and exclaimed, "Frank, you're going to be the death of me yet! You can go, but if you get hit by a car, or if anything happens to you, don't tell anyone where you came from."

On July 5, 1973, Ann Duer arrived at the hospital to transport Dad and me to the airport for the red-eye flight to Dayton. It was with more than a small amount of trepidation that I boarded the plane, for I feared that I would suddenly find that this wasn't actually real, but only the side effects of the medication I was taking. Leaving everyone who had made such an impact on my life was also very difficult.

Our flight was uneventful, and we landed at the airport at 6:00 a.m. The first one to greet me was my sister who hugged me, declaring, "I love you, and missed you very much." I looked at Mom and wondered what she was thinking. She later told me that she was speechless. It had only been a short while ago that she had visited me to find no change in my condition. It was beyond her imagination that I could have progressed so far in such a short time.

When we arrived in Coldwater, it had just begun to rain, and while riding through the main street of the town, I remember seeing one of the ladies who worked at the five and dime store sweeping the sidewalk. I rolled down the window and yelled, "Girlie, it's me, Frank! I'm home and cured!" She threw her broom into the air and exclaimed, "Hooray!" We proceeded on to the trailer to meet Grandma, who reacted with disbelief, and could only remark that her couch seemed strange without my occupying it. Because I didn't want Grandma to know that I smoked, I left for a short time and took a walk around the block. On the way, I encountered two women on their front porch who welcomed me home and asked, "Aren't you glad to be home and not in the city?" I answered, "No, I fell in love with New York and some day plan to live there. I guess there are bad areas everywhere, but New York seems to have more of them because of its size."

For some reason, it seemed that I had been away for 20 years, and I felt like a complete stranger in the town in which I had grown up. It still seemed as if the past several days were a product of my imagination, and I would soon find myself back in New York City.

Chapter IX

The following months were spent renewing old acquaintances and rejoicing in my recovery. Many of these friends wrote to me every week of my hospitalization, and it was imperative that I personally thank them all. Getting back into the everyday life that I had known, however, was not that easy, and my first outing proved how my life had changed. Driving around town and seeing how much beer could be consumed was not my idea of a good time. Again I felt like a stranger in my home- town, even though it was great to feel normal.

Meanwhile, since I was unable to be employed, my mother visited the Social Security Office to get me on disability. To her dismay, she was informed that there was no such illness as Tourette Syndrome listed in their medical journals. Mom finally wrote to Dr. Sweet who confirmed my diagnosis, and I began receiving a monthly check. Besides receiving $180 a month, my medications were all paid for, so I gave my parents $80 a month for room and board, and managed to get by on what was left. When I found myself with too much idle time, Dr. Beare recommended that I try to work somewhere part time. A good friend of our family owned the local supermarket and offered me a job in his store starting at the minimum wage. Thinking that I was not permitted to earn that much, I told him that I would settle for one dollar an hour. Working was a new experience for me, but with all the medication I was on, I became very exhausted after only a few hours. Eventually I had to settle for three hours of work on Thursdays and Fridays.

Mom had also talked to the organist at church, and I began playing for some of the services. Our church had just purchased a new Allen digital electronic organ, and I was thrilled to get my fingers on that piece of equipment. For a while, I played twice a week, and that fall, joined the adult choir. By then I was on Haldol and Cogentin daily, and Darvon Cpd as needed for severe leg pain that resulted from taking Cogentin. I had a terrible time staying awake past eight p.m., and soon had to drop out of the choir.

Besides the lethargy and pain there were other side effects of the drugs. Probably the worst of these was the inability to urinate. I would have to stand barefoot on the cold floor with the faucet running, and concentrate for about ten minutes before getting relief. This went on for about six to seven months before abating.

Everyone was glad that I was "cured" and back home, but somehow I felt alone, and left out of things Perhaps they were all afraid to be associated with someone who had an illness they didn't understand. During that time, I did remain free from those horrible tics, and was thankful for that.

In 1972 the TSA (Tourette Syndrome Association) was formed as a nonprofit organization for research and public education. I was one of the first persons to join in the hope of finding an end to this madness. Dad and I returned to New York for a conference in 1974, and had blood drawn for research. They were trying to find a common bond that would link the two of us to the disease.

Finally in the fall of 1975 I began going out socially again. Because I wanted to fit in, I drank an occasional beer in spite of all my medication. I'll never know what precipitated the slow return of my tics about two years later. Instead of the flinging about of my arms and legs, they were more in the form of vocalizations, "Huh! Huh! Huh! Huh!", touching others, or picking at my skin. I felt as if another curse had invaded my body, and friends tended to shy away from me for fear of being poked or pinched. I was desperate to be accepted, and would have done anything to fit in with the crowd.

There were, however, positive events occurring in my life at that time. I had met some new friends, Jerry Kessen and Dan Eckstein, who worked with me. I began waiting around for them until the store closed with the hope of becoming part of their crowd. Thank God it worked, and eventually I also met Larry Westgerdes and Rick Rutschilling. They were great friends, and befriended me in spite of all my symptoms. My attempts at explaining TS to them weren't too successful, and when we met people they would explain my actions by saying, "This is Frank. He arps." Every Friday we attended the high school football game, and after the game, usually migrated to the local bar for several pitchers of beer. I hated beer, but consumed enough of it to finally acquire a taste for it. In time we progressed to drinking wine, and that was more to my liking, especially one called Boone's Farm.

One weekend we drove to Cincinnati, Ohio, for a ball game. The rest of the clan brought beer, but I brought two bottles of Boone's Farm, and proceeded to drink one entire bottle by the time we were about forty miles from our destination. They stopped to use the rest room in Hamilton and when they came out, could not find me. They were yelling, "Where's Bone?" (Bone was a nickname they had given me.) In spite of my yelling as loud as possible, I was not heard, and eventually they found me under a bush purging Boone's Farm from my body Although I couldn't find any humor in my situation, they all thought it was very funny, and never let me forget about it. I can assure you that Boone's Farm wine ceased to be my favorite, and I never drank it again.

As we neared Cincinnati, we were caught in a traffic jam for about an hour, and everyone was desperately in need of a rest room. There was a huge hill beside us, and I suggested that we climb the mountain and get relief there. Three of us must have had more to drink than the others, so we crawled up the hill and with the accompaniment of blaring horns and shouting, clapping people, relieved ourselves. We were extremely fortunate that there were no state troopers in the area, as we most certainly would have spent the night in jail. As it was, we all crawled back into the car, and made it to the ball game. I don't think any of us cared or knew the outcome of the game, but we did feel glad to get home that night.

My parents were sick with disappointment when my tics reappeared, and things again began deteriorating at home. By that time we were all becoming accustomed to living more normal lives when all the ugly symptoms began returning.

A new physician, an internist, had just moved to the area, so I began consulting him. He said that I needed a good paddling and a hot woman who wanted sex twenty-four hours a day. On his recommendation, I began sessions with a female psychologist, and I met with her for several years. Because of the complexity of the symptoms of Tourette Syndrome, she was unable to offer me any way to cope with them.

I had developed a hernia in high school, so with the relapse of my disease and the stress we were all under at home, I made arrangements for its repair. At that time such surgery entailed at least three to five days of hospitalization, and would give us all some respite from each other. When it was time to be dismissed from the hospital, I fought desperately to stay, but was unsuccessful. I dreaded going back to a home where I no longer felt welcome, but there was no other alternative.

After surgery I returned to work at the supermarket, only to run into more problems there. Because of the effects of all my medication, it was almost impossible to carry out heavy loads of groceries. One day I dropped an entire load of ice cream, sending it rolling across the floor. After discussing my problems with my parents, the manager of the market gave me my walking papers. I was very offended at the time, but today fully understand his decision.

All my friends were leaving for school or for better jobs, so I began hanging out with my doctor and some of his pals. He owned several pet cats, and was going to attend a conference for a week, so I agreed to stay in his home and care for them. He came to get me at 11:00 on a Sunday night, and after I had gotten into the car, said, "Don't ask questions. I have a lady friend staying overnight."

What a surprise that lady friend was! She was a very beautiful, voluptuous woman with perfect hair and makeup. The doctor left early the next morning, and his lady friend also disappeared. That was not to be the last of her, however, as every night there would be a tap on the door or window, accompanied by a sexy voice saying, "Frankie, it's me. Let me in." There was no doubt in my mind what she wanted, but she didn't get it from me. I went home on the following Monday, and to this day I wonder what it would have been like if I'd let her into the house.

In April of that year, against severe objections from my mom, I applied for a full-time job in a local factory. Mom felt that it would be impossible to work all the hours demanded of me in the factory since I couldn't even fulfill the needs of a part time job at the supermarket. In spite of her protests and with the help of a family friend, three weeks later I began working full time at the New Idea factory. I was in charge of incoming and outgoing mail, and drove a small cart to various areas at the plant to pick up and make deliveries. Unfortunately my lack of coordination, coupled with the incessant tics, caused many dents in the cart's fenders. I was also the target of practical jokes from the plant workers, such as a dead rat on the cart seat, grease on the steering wheel, and other mean tricks. I'll admit that I did not know how to handle their sense of humor, and have never forgotten how insensitive some people are to one less fortunate than they. Within a short time my tics got worse and I started to forget what was to be picked up and where it was to be taken.

Because of the disruption the return of my symptoms was causing my family, and the fact that I was receiving a regular salary, I moved into an apartment. It was good to be independent, but at times it became unbearably lonely. Luckily, the tenants were very kind and none of them complained about my tics which were becoming worse every day.

That winter some of my friends asked me to go skiing with them, and against my better judgement, I braved the cold and went with them. Climbing the hill to get to the ski lift was such a chore that I kept falling backward into the snow. The following day I woke with a fever of 103 degrees. I felt like dying, and crawled into bed prepared to do so. That evening my doctor and one of his male friends arrived at my apartment with a supply of whiskey and pot insisting that I try some to help my sore throat. When I refused, they said, "Let's get the fuck out of here! He's no fun!" Eventually the good doctor told me that he no longer wanted me as a patient because I wasn't going to change. That was probably one of the better turns that life dealt me, as I probably would have fallen into the habit of using drugs and alcohol, further worsening the problems I already had.

During this time another problem had been emerging. I became obsessed with my diagnosis, and lost interest in every other topic of conversation. I had Tourette Syndrome, and nothing else mattered. Almost every day I visited the Kanney household, seeking consolation and encouragement from them. No matter what housework she was doing, Marilyn would stop and listen to me, and I would relentlessly follow her around the house. One of her friends described my actions this way, "Frank could be standing in my living room complaining about his illness and if a horse walked in, he would not even notice it!"

After a while Marilyn became upset with my entire attitude. She told me that she was tired of being my cheerleader, and didn't want to see me again until I had something positive to discuss. I suppose that was a tough love type of thing, but I just thought that she too had abandoned me, and I was very upset. I left her house very despondent and when I had walked a short distance, the husband of a friend of the family passed me in his car. He stopped and asked if I wanted a ride, and I agreed to go with him. He then asked what I had planned for the day, and when I said that I had no plans, he suggested that I go home with him. Since I was visibly upset, I thought that he probably saw this and could offer me some solace.

Well, his particular solace was not at all what I had in mind. At first he was very kind, and made me feel as if he were really interested in my problems. But this was followed with erotic innuendos, and ended with mutual sexual release. I'll never understand why I was coerced into his plan, but once it was ended, I left with an immense feeling of guilt, and knew that I was too ashamed to ever tell anyone about this. I'm sure he knew the effect it would have on me, as his advances continued for a long time. There was no way I could stop them short of telling my parents what was happening and getting drawn into a huge scandal. I was finally released from his abuse when he moved out of town. Although he was gone, he left a horrible feeling of self disgust and guilt with me that will never go away.

Shortly after that I met Sister Jane Francis, a nun who was an LPN working at the nursing home. I was practicing the piano for a spring program that was to be held there when she walked by and said, "Hi, Frank." It was such a pleasure to see a nun dressed in a white habit that after she introduced herself, I invited her to have breakfast with me. It was the beginning of another great friendship. Besides offering me much moral support, she helped clean my apartment and offered comfort in many ways. We drove to her home in Kentucky where I met her mother and again was welcomed into a great home atmosphere.

Chapter X

In February of 1979 I was sent back to New York to be placed on an experimental medication. Dr. Shapiro was no longer associated with New York Hospital so I was admitted to Mt. Sinai. Again they ran numerous tests, and scheduled me for a CT scan. When we arrived at the x-ray department they informed me that I had to surrender the rosary that was clamped in my hands. I remember giving them quite a battle about this, but eventually they won and the scan was completed. I don't recall the name of the experimental medication, but it was completely ineffective in controlling my symptoms, and I developed severe diarrhea from it.

I stayed at that hospital for one month, and became very depressed because of another treatment failure. All the tests and medication were of no use, and I felt as if I were a regular person locked in Tourette Syndrome, never to find the key to getting out. During that hospitalization, an older nurse, Anatolia Nobleza, befriended me. We went to the St. Patrick's Day parade one Sunday, and the St. Thomas Moore Church the next. We corresponded until 1984 when her brother died suddenly from a heart attack, and she went back to the Phillipine Islands to recover from severe depression. I have not heard from her since she left.

When I arrived home, Mom didn't want me to return to work in the factory, so they were generous and gave me a job cleaning the executive mansion across the street from the plant. I worked five hours every evening, receiving a decent pay check plus insurance benefits. The job was good, but I had increased my dosage of Haldol and occasionally fell asleep on the job. More than once I got caught dozing, and it's a wonder that I didn't get fired. Eventually the work became too exhausting, so I quit and went back on disability.

My next confinement was in Riverside Hospital in Columbus. Initially I was processed through the emergency room because no hospital beds were available. We waited there from 4:00 to 9:00 p.m. before being admitted to a neurological floor. I greeted the nurses on the unit by barking one large tic. A nurse who was in the hallway with her medication tray was so startled that her tray flew into the air, spilling all of her pills. She shouted, "What the hell was that?" When I explained that I had Tourette Syndrome, she asked, "What in God's name is Tourette Syndrome?"

I knew that this place would not be the answer to my prayers, but they would certainly become acquainted with a patient with Tourette Syndrome. During this stay, I was placed on 80 to 100 mg of Haldol, and couldn't get out of bed. As a consequence, I developed cysts on my rear, and had to have them excised in bed.

Before my discharge a nurse came into the room and said, "I think your future lies in a monastery on the West Coast to calm you down. Sell all your possessions and join the Hindu order." In retrospect, I wonder if she could have been right. I may have prevented the hell that my life became in future years.

That fall Orrin called with some unbelievable news. He had met an actor by the name of Tom Noonan who had become intrigued with his illness and the problems associated with it. He was interested in making a movie about Tourette Syndrome, and wanted to interview me.

Tom arrived in November in the middle of a snowstorm. He did not have a license to drive and borrowed the car of his girl friend, Susan Sarandon. On the way, the car slid into a ditch, and because of his lack of a driver's license, he simply waited until the morning when he was spotted by a truck driver who pulled him out. His first task upon getting here was to go to the local florist and order flowers for Susan and let her know that he had arrived safely. Tom stayed for four days, and while he was here, he followed me around, constantly asking about my past, what it's like having Tourette Syndrome, and how other people dealt with it. Some evenings I had to beg him to let me go to bed because I was too exhausted from all the effects of my medication. My parents took him out to eat one evening, but for some reason, I was not invited to go with them.

One of the local papers wrote an article about Tom and me and the "special hell" that Tourette victims endure. Tom compared it to throwing up or a hiccup. You can suppress it for a while, but eventually it comes out. The more you hold it in, the more violent it becomes.

Tom went back to New York City, but returned in December shortly before Christmas and stayed for three days. We visited some of the area hang-outs, and again I was barraged with questions. Before he left, he gave me Susan Sarandon's address and phone number, and I talked to her on the phone once in a while. Tom called occasionally for several months, but the phone calls eventually stopped, and the movie never materialized.

In the meantime, my tics had graduated to picking at my head and legs, causing painful bleeding sores. My vocalizations graduated to echoing the speech of others. "Why! Why! Why! Well! Well! Well!", on and on, were constantly heard from me, so I again consulted my psychiatrist, who was still unable to help me. For several months I had considered quitting my job to attend college, and with her assistance, I passed the test to qualify myself for BVR (Bureau of Vocational Rehabilitation). By passing the test, I received free tuition and books, so I quit my job and became a student at a branch of Wright State University in Celina. My classes were English, Sociology, and Psychology.

In high school I had met an extraordinary girl named Dru Kuenning from nearby Celina. She was dating one of my friends, but for some reason, we became pals. One day she invited me for dinner at her home, and when I objected because of my symptoms she said, "No, I'll explain your disease to my parents and they will understand." They certainly did understand, and made me feel more than welcome, never once seeming to take notice of my tics. Their home became a blessing for me when I was attending Wright State, as they offered me the use of their house to sleep whenever I became too tired to drive home. Many times I stopped after class and slept there before going back to Coldwater.

Unfortunately this was at the time before help was available for anyone with learning disabilities, so in spite of working myself silly, I earned only C's and D's in college. No matter how hard I tried, I couldn't comprehend what was taught, and when the classes were over, I remembered nothing about their content. After several months I met with my counselor who informed me that I was wasting the state's money and recommended that I quit.

Since I was no longer working, the rent for my present apartment became too costly, so I had to make other living arrangements. Moving back home was out of the question as Dad and Mom were adamant about this. I felt as if they had completely abandoned me, and when I questioned them about it some years later, they explained that they wanted Teresa to grow up in a normal house where she could entertain her friends and not become embarrassed with me.

My uncle, Jim Noll, owned some apartments where the rent was more within our reach, so when one became available, I moved into one of them. I was very unhappy with this change, but was assured that the move was only on a trial basis. Shortly after I arrived, one of the tenants observed some of my tics in action, and asked if he could do anything to help. If only he could have!

Life in that apartment was lonelier than it had ever been, as all of my friends were getting married, and I was not accepted at home. In order to make it more bearable, I began visiting various friends and relatives shortly before they sat down to their evening meal. They would usually invite me to eat with them, and since I had no money to buy food, their generosity sustained me.

My cousin, Mary Jo Bruggeman often stopped by to visit. She would greet me with a big hug, and always assured me that I was welcome in her home anytime, tics and all. It was hard to accept the fact that I was tolerated in her home, but not in my own. I'm sorry to say that in time I came to hate my parents. I realized that they were trying to make me independent, but all

I wanted was to be with my family and feel their love. This, however, was not to be accomplished until much later in life, and I continued with my bleak existence.

Dad and Mom had not stopped hoping for more control of my symptoms, so that summer I was admitted to Otto C. Epp Hospital in Kenwood, a suburb of Cincinnati. I was under the impression that I was to be admitted to the neurological department of the hospital, and was irate when I was confined to a psychiatric floor under the care of a husband and wife team. Dad was with me during the interview with them and became very disgusted with their attitudes. At one point I became very loud, and the wife said, "Frank, you don't have to make those tics to get my attention." By this time Dad had reached the end of his patience and proclaimed, "Listen, you bitch! He has Tourette Syndrome, and we came down here for help!" Before I was dismissed from the hospital, he told them both, "You two were meant for each other. You're both fucking goofy!"

It had been discovered that a blood pressure medication called Catapress was effective in controlling some of the symptoms of Tourette patients so the dosage of Haldol was drastically reduced, and I was started on the Catapress regimen. This meant that my blood pressure had to be closely monitored until a suitable dosage could be found, thus prolonging my stay at that institution. Again, the medication seemed to have no effect on my symptoms, leaving me with another failure!

I did gain one thing from that hospitalization. Most of my fellow patients used profanity as a second language, and for some reason the word, "Fuck" became imbedded in my mind. Until then, my coprolalia consisted of outbursts of a few choice words, but after that confinement I began to shout explosively, "Fuck! Fu—Fuck!" unwillingly. Attempts at replacing it with something more acceptable were unsuccessful, and I'm still plagued with it. You can understand the consternation of my family and friends when I began using "fuck" as a regular part of my vocabulary! Believe me when I tell you that I've uttered that infernal word with all conceivable inflections—loud, explosive, high, low, long, short, etc.

Three weeks after being dismissed from the hospital I had to return so the medication Catapress could be discontinued and I could start back on Haldol. My cousin, Carol accompanied Dad and me, and I shook so violently the entire trip that the car began shaking. After a while Dad couldn't stand it, so Carol took over and drove the rest of the way. During this hospitalization my roommate was a large black man who was in rehabilitation for drug and alcohol abuse. Fortunately my frequent utterances of, "Nigger!Nigger!" did not phase him, or I may not be around today. I was dismissed in time to attend the community picnic, and was looking forward to attending it. An incident occurred that weekend that sent me into one of the worst depressions I've ever had. My sister was bringing her boyfriend's parents to meet Dad and Mom, so Mom thought it would be better if I stayed in Grandma's trailer while they visited. Mom had prepared for that day months in advance by cleaning everything until it was spotless, cooking up a storm, and doing everything to make a good impression on Teresa's future in-laws.

When I arrived at the picnic, I spotted Mom and made eye contact with her, only to have her ignore my presence completely. In a rage I turned away, ran home, and cried bitterly. After I reached my apartment, the entire thought of what my existence had become was more than I could bear and I pounded my fist against the wall until it gave way, becoming as my life, a large deep hole that I was rapidly sinking into. I felt as if I'd been rejected by the one person who always stood by me. This episode precipitated a time of deep regression. I stopped eating, bathing, and literally withdrew from the world, and no one seemed to care.

One day Dru Kuenning stopped by to see how I was doing and found me in a deplorable condition. When she heard that I had been existing on cookies and water, she took me home with her. Her parents came to my rescue by feeding me and giving me a reason to live. The Kuennings are the epitome of true Christianity, and I'll always be indebted to them.

Another morale booster occurred when Dave and Jill Eilerman moved back to town. Dave was a true friend all through high school, and he and Jill soon included me in many of their family's activities. They eventually had three girls, and explained my illness to them as soon as they could comprehend it. As the girls got older, I babysat with them quite often, and what a time that was! One of their favorite games was make-believe -beauty shop, and I became their client. Since that was the generation when we all wore our hair longer, I was perfect for the part. They put rollers in my hair, and when they determined that it was dry, would comb it and give me a kiss. You don't get that kind of service in any salon that I ever went to. We also played school and cowboy and Indians, and in the latter game I was inevitably the Indian whom they tied to a tree. They always became ecstatic when I couldn't get loose and had to ask for help.

I've always been able to count on Dave and he is like the brother I never had. During the years of my sexual abuse, he was the only one with whom I could confide. After each episode I would call him to remorsefully confess my transgression, and he would assure me that I was not the guilty party but was being used by someone else for his wrongdoing. I carried so much guilt from each incident that without Dave, I probably would have ended my life.

We have our disagreements at times, especially on religious matters. Even though I was raised in a strict Catholic atmosphere, I still struggle with my faith at times. Dave joined another church, but we remain good friends, and have learned much from each other. I firmly believe that in the end, our fate is going to be determined by how we have led our lives on earth, and not on one religious denomination. Dave and his family represent the Christianity that is necessary for eternal life in heaven.

Chapter XI

In 1980 I met Lois Hammond, who has a daughter with severe Tourette Syndrome. Lois was opening the Ohio Chapter for Tourettte Syndrome, and through her I became active in the society. One of our projects entailed selling huge cookies for $1.00 per cookie. I sold over 100 of them and received an award for being the year's best volunteer. We also presented programs at the local hospital and nursing home, educating the employees and administration about the devastating effects of the disease, hoping to give them a better understanding of the actions of an individual with Tourette Syndrome.

Our next endeavor was to sell raffle tickets for a car, but because of limited funds, the best we could afford was a five or six- year- old Ford. Everyone was too embarrassed to sell the tickets, and that was not a very successful venture.

Lois became very busy with her demanding jobs as director of the Tourette Association and caring for her daughter Lisa. Lisa frequently became violent, throwing and smashing things, slamming her fists into the wall, etc. Because of her erratic behavior, Lois's husband became very defensive of Lisa's actions when they were outside the home. If they were in a restaurant and people stared at her because of her gyrations, he would declare, "Listen! My daughter has Tourette Syndrome, and if you continue to stare at her, I have a gun in the car that could put an end to that."

The family eventually moved to Tennessee in an area near Dolly Parton's birthplace, and Lois and Lisa became born again Christians. Quite often during the services they would explain Lisa's illness to the congregation, and Lisa, who was blessed with a beautiful voice, sang for them. Remarkably, she also exhibited no symptoms while singing. She soon became a country gospel singer, achieved great success, and went off disability. Subsequently, she was invited to Japan, and gave a concert there, giving them great insight into Tourette Syndrome.

Father Wehrle, the pastor of the nearby parish of Philothea, offered me a job playing the organ at his church on Sundays and for weddings and funerals. The parish is very small, so I enjoyed the experience very much. Father was very kind to me, but unfortunately he died from a cerebral aneurism several years later.

Since I wasn't getting any relief from my symptoms, I became involved in an organization at church entitled, Christ Renews His Parish. I was again hoping that by becoming spiritually involved, I would miraculously be cured. This led to my becoming a member of the Charismatic Team at Maria Stein, Ohio. It was there that everyone spoke in tongues, but try as I might, I couldn't do the same. I did manage to fool everyone for a while by reciting some Latin phrases learned when I was an altar boy in grade school. After this no longer worked, I again began to worry that I might be possessed by the devil, and expressed this thought to some of the members. They recommended a trip to the small town of Mendon, Ohio, where we met with an old man in his home who was noted by many to get rid of evil spirits. After introductions, this gentleman declared that I was indeed possessed by the devil, and began praying over me shouting, "Be healed in the name of Jesus Christ! Do you believe that Jesus is your savior, and can cure you?" Of course I did and made a loud strange noise in agreement. This quieted the old man, and halfway through the meeting, I fell asleep. Everyone thought that perhaps I had been cured, but eventually came to realize that my medication had kicked in, and I slept from exhaustion.

I was undaunted, and continued to read all the books on healing that I could find. Finally I went with the organization's members to a church in Lima, Ohio, for a healing service. We got into our pews and I confided to my friend, "I don't think I should be here." She said, "Just calm down and pray." Soon a nun came out and we all began to pray the rosary together. Imagine their embarrassment when every "Ave" from me consisted of "Hail Mary, fuck-fuck-fuck of grace." Of course the poor nun had no idea where this blasphemy originated, and continued with her prayer. Later when the priest arrived and sprinkled holy water on us, I confessed to him that all those "fucks" were coming from me, and I couldn't help it. He was then determined to exorcize the demon from me, and continued to sprinkle the water again, shouting, "Be healed in the name of Jesus Christ!" And I yelled, "More! More!" After several minutes of this, my cries changed to, "It's not working!" Soon he stopped and asked, "Do you feel any better?" I answered, "No, but I have to go to the bathroom!" That ended the exorcism.

In 1983 my sister went to college in Cincinnati, Ohio, leaving a big void in Mom's life. I still lived in an apartment, but much of my time was spent visiting with Grandma Miller and doing errands for her. She became my main support, and would shout "shut up!" when my tics got excessively loud. Fortunately for me, her hearing was nearly gone, and I didn't get reprimanded as often as I should.

Later that year Dad and I flew to New York for a conference with Dr. Shapiro to find if there had been any advances in the treatment of Tourette Syndrome. He informed us that the disease seems to originate in the basil ganglia of the brain, but so far no additional treatment could be found for it. In other words my choices remained the same. I could stay off medication, become educated and continue with all the same symptoms, or stay on medication but because of its side effects, be ineffective in the work field.

While in New York we visited with Susan Bloch who was still fighting her own losing battle with kidney failure. We were fortunate to meet Ellen Zeisler, Susan's second in command, and instantly felt a kinship with her. When Dad discovered that he hadn't brought enough money with him to get home, Ellen immediately came to his rescue with a loan to cover our expenses. We have remained friends ever since that day, and Ellen has certainly gone beyond the call of duty by encouraging me to write this book.

About this time, Grandma went to California to visit. After two months, she became homesick and returned home. Her health had been slowly deteriorating, and she was eventually admitted to the Intensive Care Unit of the local hospital. Her cardiologist felt that she definitely needed a pacemaker, but true to form, Grandma wanted no part of that. She told him, "I have five-hundred dollars in my pocketbook that you can have if you get me the hell out of here." After much family discussion, she was transferred to the nursing home and I moved into her trailer.

Dad visited her every night for nineteen months, and every Sunday Mom cooked her a big breakfast containing all her favorite foods. She especially liked bacon, and when I'd tell her that it would clog her arteries, she would say, "At my age, who cares! I've been eating like this all my life, and it's too late to change." Grandma died in July of 1987 at the age of 90. She willed her trailer to me, and that became my home.

Chapter XII

In 1987 my sister got married. She kindly asked me to be in her wedding, but because of my worsening tics and OCD, I had to refuse. Following their wedding she and her husband settled in Cincinnati, and we didn't see each other for some time. Our never becoming close was another tragic result of my repulsive disease, as she had to endure as much ridicule as I did. On many occasions she would be confronted by tormentors with, "There's the doggie's sister!" and "How's your brother, the dog?" It was unfortunate that most people considered my symptoms to be psychological and could be controlled by me if I really tried.

Every distasteful individual, however, had another counterpart who made a difference in my life. Some of them were the physicians and nurses who became my friends. Nearly every evening I ate dinner at the hospital cafeteria and would occasionally meander into the emergency room to converse with the nurses. For some reason I always felt at ease there because they all tried to understand my illness, and made me feel like a human being.

In the fall of that year the National Tourette Association meeting was held in Cincinnati, Ohio, and we all attended. Sister Jane Francis is from Kentucky, just across the river from Cincinnati, so she drove my car and we stayed with her mother. Dad and Mom drove separately and spent the weekend with Teresa and Jim. We all met on Sunday morning and participated in some very good sessions. Orrin, my former roommate in the New York Hospital, gave an excellent presentation and it was great to see him again. He has been a success story for all the physicians who knew and treated him because of the fact that he became a thriving physician in spite of his affliction.

One of the highlights of this convention was my meeting with Dr. Oliver Sacks, a noted neurologist who has done much work studying how individuals survive and adapt to different neurological diseases and conditions. He wrote many books about these diseases and their effects on the human brain and mind. In his first book, "The Man Who Mistook His Wife for a Hat," he described patients struggling to live with conditions ranging from Tourette Syndrome to autism, Parkinson's disease, hallucinations, phantom limb syndrome, schizophrenia, and Alzheimer's disease.

In 1966 when he was the consulting neurologist for Beth Abraham Hospital, Dr. Sacks encountered a group of patients who had spent decades in strange frozen states unable to move. Apparently they were all survivors of encephalitis and were inflicted with the disease from 1916 to 1927. Dr. Sacks treated these patients with large doses of the drug L-dopa, a drug more familiarly known today as dopamine, which is the drug of choice for Parkinsonism. After this treatment, the patients all came back to life. Sadly, their reincarnation was short lived, and they all reverted back to their comatose state.

In 1977 Dr. Sacks wrote the book "Awakening" about this experience. Harold Pinter, a play-writer, was inspired by the book and produced a play, "A Kind of Alaska," and then the movie, "Awakenings," starring Robert DeNiro and Robin Williams. The movie was met with much acclaim and is still recommended viewing for all. I introduced myself to Dr. Sacks, explaining that I was a big fan of his and had read many of his books. We conversed for nearly an hour, and during the course of our discussion, the f--k word escaped from me several times, prompting the Doctor to ask what order of Judaism I was from. When I explained that I was neither a Reformed nor Orthodox Jew, but a Roman Catholic, he laughed and remarked, "What a surprise! I've never before met a Catholic who was unabashed when saying the "f" word." Before he left we exchanged addresses and corresponded for about five years. His letters were very interesting, and were interspersed with pictures and stories about one of his favorite places, the Botanical Gardens in New York City.

One of the objectives of the Tourette association meeting was to educate the public about the disease and its symptoms. The need for this education was evidenced the next day when one of the men from the assemblage went across the street to a Wendy's to get some lunch. As he began to order from the menu, numerous obscenities and tics became part of his choices. His efforts at explaining his illness were not understood by the employees, so they became frightened and called the police who arrested him. Later in the afternoon the press arrived at his hotel en masse, and the write-up about the event appeared in all three Cincinnati newspapers the next day.

I contributed to this education by continuing to give talks on the disease to various organizations, encouraging donations to the society. I don't think I'll ever forget the one I gave to a group of K of C members at one of their meetings. The Knights of Columbus is an organization composed of men from the Catholic church who are devoted to the betterment of mankind. When I finished my talk I asked for a contribution to benefit the research into Tourette Syndrome. A member immediately stood, declaring that he did not think it was necessary to donate to our cause, as he thought it was included in the combined charities drive. It wasn't included in that drive, and I left empty handed. I lost all respect for that organization after that incident, as the members seemed more interested in getting their food and drink than in my plea for help for people less fortunate than they.

Chapter XIII

One day when I was visiting in the ER a young guy came through the door very casually dressed in shorts and a T-shirt, and when I went to the cafeteria to eat my meal, he gave me a big hello and asked if he could sit with me. My first thought was, "Wow! This man is really friendly for being a complete stranger." To my surprise, he said nothing about my actions, and I was further amazed when some of the employees entering the cafeteria addressed him as "Doctor." I later learned that he was one of the physicians who worked in the ER several days a week, and his name was Gary Huber. This was certainly unusual, as I was accustomed to doctors being somewhat standoffish, and he definitely did not fit into that category. I wondered what he thought of my actions, but in the ensuing weeks the nurses must have explained my illness to him. He always found time to talk with me, and it was the beginning of a lasting friendship.

Gary has a way of teasing me about Tourette Syndrome without belittling me, and not many people have that ability. Whenever the nurses told him I was waiting for him, he would loudly greet me with, "Fu-Fu-Fu-Frank's waiting! How's Fraaaaaank? How are your tic-tic-tics today?" or some other nonsense. I'll never forget the time that he came to my trailer to visit, and noting that I was feeling especially low that day, suggested that we get something to eat. My tics were very bad, and he said that I needed to get some fresh air and a change of scenery to lift my spirits. I finally agreed to go to Bettie's Restaurant with him after he said that every time I had a tic, he would tic louder so the people would think all that noise was coming from him. I never thought he would follow through with that plan, but sure enough, after my first "whoop." he countered with one louder and longer than mine. As if that weren't enough, a very well endowed girl walked into the restaurant and I brought her to his attention. That proved to be the wrong thing to do, as he kept saying the word "tits" over and over quietly until it forced me to tic the word "tits" loud enough for the entire place to hear it. We had quite a time during that meal laughing and behaving idiotically.

It was very quiet one evening in the ER when Gary and I began clowning around. We soon began to argue which one of us was the stronger. I said, "There is no question about it, Gary. I'm taller, and could beat you in a minute." "Try it, Frank." he challenged, and with that, grabbed me and proceeded to squeeze me hard. I fought and fought to no avail, and finally fell to the floor. I must have hit my head on the door frame because there was blood on my hand when I straightened my hair. I threw a fit when Gary informed me that it would require two to three staples to repair the damage. Since he had proven that he could handle me, I agreed to the treatment. Of course he had to rub it in that he was the stronger, and I had to admit that he surprised me with his strength.

Eventually Gary began working more hours in the ER, so in order to save driving time, he rented a small house in a neighboring town. I helped him move into the house, and on some of the days when he was off duty, he invited me over. The coffee pot was always on, and I made sure that we had enough cigarettes. On quite a few occasions, he invited me to drive with him to Cincinnati to visit with his family who proved to be as friendly and accommodating as he was.

The first Christmas after our meeting, he announced that he had a gift for me. That evening there was a knock on my trailer door, and there he stood holding a large beautiful package. He handed it to me and said, "Merry Christmas." Besides being merry, that Christmas was also very warm, because the package contained the nicest coat, gloves, and scarf that I'd ever owned.

At times I also became the caretaker of Inker, Gary's dog. When Gary had to work overnight in the ER, I had the job of feeding him. The dog was the love of his life, and often made the trip to Cincinnati with us.

One winter the doctors from the ER gave a Christmas party. It was held in one of their homes, and Gary invited me to go with him as his guest. After we got there, I felt like an outsider, and told him that I felt completely out of place. Gary immediately took me outside and said, "Look, I invited you because I wanted you to be here. You're as welcome as any other person, so you may as well go back in there and enjoy yourself." I did enjoy myself that evening, and again received a much needed boost in my confidence from him.

Although I knew that Gary would eventually move to bigger and better things, it was hard to accept when he announced that he was moving to Columbus to further his training as an ER physician. He assured me that we would always remain friends, and has been true to his word. When it became necessary for me to buy a car he lent me the money to do so, with the stipulation that I did not have to worry about paying him back. That gave me all the incentive I needed to work harder, and I did manage to pay off the loan. Not many people are blessed with a friend who does so much for him, and is always there when needed.

I was fairly satisfied with the family physician I was seeing until he wrote a letter to a local newspaper about his views on sexuality, abortion, and morals. Some of his views were very conflicting with mine, so I felt that I needed a change. Dr. Masser was on staff at the hospital and I had talked to him in the past. When he agreed to meet with me to discuss the contents of that letter, he was so sincere and helpful that I immediately felt relaxed and asked him to be my doctor. His consent finally gave me someone to regulate my medication, listen intelligently to my problems, and offer hope, though little, that the future may soon be better. I have bent his ear so often over the years that it's a wonder that he hasn't discharged me a long time ago.

Later that year a friend offered to drive me to a seminar on Tourette Syndrome that was held in Cincinnati. Shortly after we arrived, I began to hear someone nearby exhibiting all sorts of tics. As it got progressively worse, my curiosity got the better of me, and I turned around to see who was making all that noise. To my surprise, about two rows behind us sat Gary with a big grin on his face. We sat through a very educational talk by Dr. David Cummings about Tourettes and how it is related to many other abnormalities.

After the meeting we all decided that some light entertainment was needed, so Gary suggested that we go to the Brass Ass. That was some entertainment! It turned out to be a strip club, and after several drinks I was really into the fun. I must admit that it was probably as educational as the seminar, but in very different ways. Gary eventually left us at our hotel room with the understanding that he would meet us the following morning at nine o'clock. Well, nine o'clock arrived and Gary didn't show. Since my friend had to be home, he checked out early and I waited. It got to be past check-out time, so I called his parents, who came to get me. It was 1:45 p.m. before he arrived home with the excuse that his watch had stopped.

The following spring our pastor arrived at the trailer and offered me a job for several hours a week during the summer. It involved helping to clean the rectory, church, and school. It sounded great to me, and after I found that it would not pay enough to interfere with my monthly disability check, I agreed to take that job in addition to playing the organ in church part time. I worked for Dave Hart, who proved to be a great boss. The job was not that difficult, but many times I had to be awakened in the morning because of the effects of my medications. Dave was very patient with me, and I was treated as if I were one of the staff. We were all invited to a Christmas party, and received a gift from the parish for all our work. About four months later I found that besides the work, the job had quite a bit of baggage associated with it. I have many memories, both good and bad of those years, and the worst of them will never be revealed.

Before Dave left to work for the Honda Corporation, he told Father, "Whatever you do, keep that job open for Frank. He can be a real klutz at times, but works very hard to do his work well." In 1992, a new priest was assigned to our parish. I quit my janitorial work, but continued my job as organist.

Two of my favorite people are Tom and Cindy Huston who owned a bike shop at the edge of Coldwater. I was interested in buying a bike, and had approached Dave about a good place to buy one. He directed me to their establishment, and after buying a bike, I began to hang around the shop. At the time I was almost chain-smoking, and Tom reprimanded me, telling me that I could not smoke that much while visiting in their shop. After arriving home, I wrote them a letter explaining how it was very difficult for me to meet new friends, and I sometimes overstayed my welcome in order to keep them. About a week later I went back to the shop, and Tom informed me that I was welcome any time. Several weeks later, I took a job cleaning the shop several days a week.

Although Tom and Cindy seemed to have a great marriage, they must have had some insurmountable problems, as they eventually obtained a divorce. Tom later moved to Florida, and I still remain friends with both of them.

Chapter XIV

In 1992 my sister and her husband presented us with a lovely baby girl, and I was honored by being her godfather. She was so small and beautiful, and during the baptism, my main concern was that I would drop her. In the course of time she was welcomed by two little sisters, and my thoughts were, "Thank goodness that girls are less likely to develop Tourette Syndrome." I pray daily that these children will not be confronted with this hardship.

Sister Catherine died in 1993. At her funeral, Father Cap, her twin brother said, "I really would like to thank all the Sisters of the Precious Blood for putting up with her for all these years. I know that she was not the most cordial person, and think she probably had mental problems. We never did get along with each other." Father Cap himself died in 1998, and by all means, that description could have been his eulogy also. Every time the two were together, Cap would chide her because she had only skipped one year of school, and he had skipped two. He said that proved he had more brains than she. Catherine must have had more brains than he knew, as she eventually earned her masters in psychology.

Catherine's views on hell probably met with much controversy in her order. An unforgettable episode was when she stood before her fellow nuns, and announced that she did not think there was a hell. She exclaimed, "I can't believe that a God who loved us enough to create us with an eternal soul, would condemn us to a hell that we could never escape!" She felt that many of us would go to a place called purgatory for a short time, but would eventually be reunited in heaven with Christ. Later in her life she developed mental problems and was unable to continue teaching. She then retired and sold real estate for several years.

In November of 1995, I again moved back home, and it was probably the start of a healing process between Mom and me. We had some good talks, and on one occasion Mom remarked that she was beginning to know me again. At last I began to feel that my parents really loved me, and that life was finally getting better.

Christmas that year proved to be very memorable as I also became reacquainted with the Kanney family and spent some time reminiscing with them. Nearly every Sunday morning, I spent time at their home, telling them about some of my past experiences. They often remarked that I should write a book about some of the crazy things that happened to me. I found all sorts of excuses why I couldn't attempt such a task, and one of them was that no one would understand my illness enough to even begin such a job. After about a year of my procrastinating, Marilyn said, "Don't give me that excuse again Frank! I'll help you write your book."

That was the beginning of quite a few years of her encouraging me to put my life into some orderly fashion so it could be chronicled. Many tears were shed in this undertaking, and we often considered discontinuing the process. However, with the encouragement of many people, we slowly made progress. I moved back into the trailer in February with the understanding that I could sleep at home whenever I wanted. That was a big break-through for us all. Shortly after that, Dr. Masser placed a call to Dr. Ruth Bruun who suggested that I start taking a medication called Anafranil. Two weeks after starting on the medication I arrived at his office in great humor, clean shaven, hair combed, and dressed fit to kill. Dr. Masser knew without asking that the medication had worked. All my tics, obsessions, and compulsions were gone, and my life began again. Occasionally the dosage had to be increased, but I felt like the luckiest person alive.

I then went on a mini vacation to visit with Gary who had finished his training and was now working in various hospitals in Cincinnati. He was amazed at how great it was to be around me without all the ridiculous antics associated with Tourettes. I also stayed with my sister and her family. We had such a good time having normal, uninterrupted conversations.

I arrived home to find that Mom and Dad were having the trailer redone, and by Labor Day I practically had a new home. Life was finally becoming normal!

After a year of normal living, Anafranil became ineffective, and all the tics, obsessions, and compulsions were back. The return of the tics also made it more complicated to live in the trailer as it was not air conditioned, and I had to leave the windows open. After several nights I was visited by a local policeman with a complaint from one of the neighbors about all the noises coming from my residence. That meant that I had to resort to sleeping with the windows closed in the middle of summer. After spending several nights of fitful sleep, Mom became aware of this and hired one of the local merchants to install an air conditioner. I came to the conclusion that if heaven is like the year of normalcy that I had experienced, all the struggling on earth will be worth it.

My luck held out when the Methodist church was in need of an organist, and I was hired for the job by Reverend Ruth Floyd. I played every Sunday for their services, and their congregation treated me as if I were a member of their family. One Sunday Reverend Ruth asked me to play for a service being held for anyone who had suffered the loss of a loved one or friend.

Various ministers, pastors, and the Hospice staff were included in the very meaningful presentation.

After the service we all met in the basement for refreshments. There I met a good friend of mine from Fort Recovery, Harriet Pearson, who introduced me to her new pastor, Tim Duther-Walls. Conversation, as usual, led to discussions about Tourette Syndrome, and he proved to be very knowledgeable about the disease. He had read every book by Dr. Oliver Sacks, and was fascinated by all the research done on Tourettes and all its related afflictions. He received his degree in theology from UC in Berkley, California, so I knew that he had a liberal mind. Tim had belonged to the Catholic church, but became disillusioned by its lack of forward movement and joined the Lutheran denomination.

I called him the following week to meet for lunch. I also invited my friend Jan Barr to join us. Jan and I had met several years before, and we frequently had lunch together. She was the director of the Red Cross in our area, on the Aid Hispanic board, and volunteered for many humanitarian projects in the church. She's always been empathetic to my problems, and is a great person to have as a friend.

The three of us had some very enlightening conversations about theology, philosophy, tradition, sexuality, etc. We learned that Tim had two children, and his wife was working on her doctorate on biblical history. He liked to tell the story of his first glimpse of Ft. Recovery. It was on the weekend of their yearly tractor pull, and after seeing all the people putting their tractors through all their gyrations, he began to wonder what he had gotten himself into.

Tim eventually came to love his congregation, and remained there for several years. I attended several services at his church and he, Jan, and I continued to meet for lunch. After one of our sessions he announced that at the end of that month he was moving to Canada. His wife Pat had accepted a teaching job in a seminary, and he in turn was offered a pastoral position in a small but growing Lutheran parish.

We continued to correspond regularly after his move until my mom's health began deteriorating, and I lost track of many of my out of state friends. Recently I received a note from him saying that he was returning to Ft. Recovery for a visit at the end of September. Since I wasn't feeling very sociable, we met at Dad and Mom's house, and talked for four hours about all the events that had occurred since our last correspondence.

The expression "when it rains, it pours" certainly began to come true in our family in 1996 and 1997. It began with Mom's forgetting little things that we all attributed to old age. This progressed with her with her putting large amounts on her charge card, something she ordinarily would not consider doing. The little things continued to get bigger so we arranged for her to have some tests done at Christ Hospital in Cincinnati. There she was diagnosed with having mild Alzheimer's disease, and placed on the medication Aricept.

She was coming to visit me one day and wrecked the car. The accident was her fault, and her one thought was that she had ruined Dad's favorite car. In the emergency room, the chief of police advised us that she should not drive again, as too many people had reported seeing her go through stop signs and stop lights. This depressed her very much, and although Dad and I let her drive in the country on occasion, it was not the same. The bicycle became her mode of transportation, and even then she ran the signs and lights. Her riding was finally relegated to the bike path that exists between Coldwater and Celina, and this went so well that we all began wondering if she really had Alzheimer's disease.

I had begun working several hours a week as a courier for the People's Bank in Coldwater. The job entailed delivering papers, etc. to their several banks in the area, and required about three hours of time. They supplied me with the car and were wonderful to work for. When Mom's affliction began, I discussed resigning because much of my time would be required to help take care of her. They were very understanding, and allowed me to keep my job and stay home whenever it became necessary.

In June Mom slipped and fell trying to get onto her bike, fracturing her right upper arm. This was the beginning of a long period of recuperation. Teresa arrived to help with her care and procured a lift chair for her. It never ceased to amaze me how Mom would respond better to a female care-giver. For over a month she had to sleep in a recliner with Dad nearby in another recliner. Two to three times a night we had to lift her onto the commode. She became very weak and refused to walk, probably for fear of falling. During this time her personality underwent a dramatic change. She became very demanding, and her language became filled with profanities she would never have thought to use before.

In July, with no progress with the therapy we were giving her, our patience was wearing thin, and we admitted her to a nursing home for physical therapy. She was there for one month and hated every minute of it. At the end of the month, we brought her home for the weekend with nurses' aides to assist. The first night she was home, she became very ill and was rushed to the hospital, admitted, and taken to surgery for a bowel resection. She stayed in the intensive care unit for six days.

Following her surgery, she was again admitted to the nursing home for four to five weeks. This admission proved successful in that she learned to walk again on her own, and fully recuperated from her surgery. Unfortunately her language got more offensive and loud, disturbing all the other residents, so we again decided to try to care for her at home. After about a year she became more confused so we enlisted the help of Home Health to give us some relief. Eventually she fell, necessitating further evaluation before the local nursing home would accept her. She was then admitted to Lima Memorial Hospital under the care of a geriatric psychiatrist for four to five weeks and then to the nursing home. The medication, Depakote, helped her considerably for a while, and we once more brought her home for a time with the help of Home Health. When the medication became ineffective, we had to transfer her back to the nursing home to stay.

Dad soon retired and began driving a van part-time for a dry -cleaning company. In a short time he became more tired, short of breath, and depressed. At first we both blamed his symptoms on his concern for Mom, but later, after developing a persistent cough, he consulted Doctor Masser. Several years before, Dad had been found to have a mitral valve prolapse, but Dr. Masser could not convince him to have an echo cardiogram. This time when his cough worsened, he had no choice but to have further evaluation and was admitted to Christ Hospital in Cincinnati. There he was diagnosed with a severe prolapse of the mitral valve and under-went surgery for replacement of the valve. After his surgery Teresa and Jim asked him to stay with them to recuperate, so when it was time to be dismissed, he moved into their home for convalescence.

During his first night there, a nurse came to check his vital signs, and found that he had a high fever. He was immediately readmitted to the hospital with a bad infection and remained there for about one month. He stayed in Cincinnati for fifty-four days, and during that time I managed to get myself into some real hot water.

Chapter XV

With Dad seriously ill in Cincinnati, I felt responsible for Mom, and visited her often at the nursing home. It was very difficult to watch her condition worsen each day and not be able to do a thing about it. All my life she never lost hope for my recovery, and I wasn't about to lose faith in hers. At times she would recognize me, but most often had to be reminded of my identity. She was on large amounts of medication to keep her quiet, and every time I went to see her, I'd find her salivating, with her head drooped down to her knees. One day when she returned to her room from the cafeteria, she still had a mouthful of food because she had forgotten to swallow.

I'm sure that I got to be a pest by persistently asking questions, but when I finally asked to speak to her doctor about her medications, etc., they replied that he would only discuss her condition with family members at his office in Lima, Ohio by appointment. That really irritated me, and out of desperation, I proclaimed, "One of these days I'm going to wring somebody's neck!"

By this time I had become fairly well acquainted with the nurses and aides, and we clowned around on occasion. That evening after seeing Mom, I went past the room where one of the nurses was preparing medications for the patients. I jokingly stuck my hand into my pocket as if I were armed, and said, "I want your drugs!" The nurse said, "Oh, you wouldn't want these drugs, Frank." We laughed together about the incident and after saying, "Goodnight," I went home.

The next day was the Tuesday before Easter, and about 9:30 a.m, I had just risen when the doorbell rang. I went to the door and was met by two policemen who immediately asked, "Did you threaten a nurse with a gun at the nursing home last night?" I replied, "No, I was just kidding around, and I'm sure she knew that. I don't even own a gun." Then they asked if I had called my mother a fucking bitch. Of course I denied that ludicrous accusation.

Finally they said, "You have two choices. You can either go to jail, or to a mental health center." I opted to go to a nearby mental health center. When they brought me home, I asked, "Can I get dressed?" Since my bedroom was in the basement, one of them followed me down and watched me dress. I was ordered into the back of the police car and escorted to the center. I don't think I have ever been so frightened in my life, and it's a wonder that they could maneuver the car with my shaking, sobbing, etc.

After we arrived I had to fill out various papers, and it was stipulated that I had to see a psychiatrist. The psychiatrist to whom I was assigned was not familiar with my case, and during the entire interview, clipped his fingernails. Then he asked, "Did I hear that you threatened to kill someone?" I explained that the statement was said only out of frustration, and he said, "I could send you to jail." I answered, "I hope not." He then said, "Well, then get out of here!" I was assigned to meet weekly with Chuck, a social worker at the center, and was dismissed.

When the policemen brought me back home, I was a mental wreck, quivering and disconsolate. The first thing I did was to call Marilyn and tell her, "I've been arrested!" After hearing what happened, she advised me to consult an attorney. The only attorney I trusted was her son-in-law, Paul, so I met with him that afternoon. He felt that a letter apologizing for my actions was in order, and he wrote a letter explaining my situation. I in turn wrote an apology. This probably stopped me from going to jail, but it certainly didn't make any points with the administrator or social worker. I was denied seeing Mom at all, even on Easter. I was also ordered not to go near their institution, or they would have me arrested.

Marilyn called the social worker at the nursing home and tried to explain the problems that I've encountered with Tourette Syndrome and its associated OCD, ADHD, tics, etc., but the social worker claimed that she knew everything there was to know about TS. Marlene Fisher, a special friend and co-worker at the bank, also called and got nowhere with her. I asked when my visiting privileges would be reinstated, and they said, "You stay out of here until we tell you to come in." They also called Dr. Masser and asked if I were violent. He assured them that I would never hurt anyone.

My weekly sessions with Chuck were great. He knew how much I dreaded going to the health center, and met with me at home. He was a very understanding individual, and we had discussions on all sorts of things. I remember one conversation where we were amazed at how people think that anyone who is different needs to see a psychiatrist. Chuck, who was very knowledgeable about TS, wrote a letter to the institution pleading my case. He received no response from that letter.

Because my funds were limited, we called the Ohio Legal Aid Society who advised me to stay calm and meet with my counselor. I explained to them that the nursing home had tapes on TS in their possession, so they called the nursing home and advised them to review the tapes they possessed. I was treated differently after that, but still did not regain my visiting privileges.

We also called the Ohio Tourette Association whose members were very familiar with my case. They sent five CDs to the administration, explaining

TS and its related tics, OCD, and ADHD. I offered to give in-services to their employees since they had said that some were afraid of me. Apparently they weren't interested, as they never took advantage of my offer.

One month later I was allowed visiting privileges on Wednesdays for one hour accompanied by the police, administrator, and social worker. They had posted a sign above Mom's bed saying, "If you see Frank abusing his mom or staying too long, report it to us." It was signed by the administrator. After two to three visits the police were excluded, but the other two remained. I brought books from World War II and discussed them and that era with Mom. It was surprising how much she remembered. She said, "I remember working in Dayton during the war making steel plates for airplanes. My sister and I shared a one-bathroom apartment with three other girls, so we rose at 5:30 every morning. On weekends we got up at the same time, played tennis, and went to church. It was hard work, but I enjoyed living in the city very much, and the war was so far away that we had no idea that such horrible things were going on in Germany. One day my dad called and said that I had to come home and take care of my mom who was very ill. My sister stayed in Dayton, and I went home to care for Mom. I've always regretted having to leave Dayton. It was so much fun."

After a time I was also allowed to call the nursing home on Monday and Friday during a specified time, but was only permitted to speak with the administrator or the social worker. Six months later, I guess everyone realized that I was going to behave, and the supervised visits were stopped. I was allowed to visit once a day at a fixed time, but was still only permitted to speak with the social worker or administrator.

One month before my probation was to end, I noticed that Mom had a persistent cough, and began to worry about her when I got home. Since this seemed to me to be a matter of importance, I called the nursing home and talked to a nurse, asking her if she would look into it. Apparently the administration was notified, and they considered that action to be a breach of my discipline, and I received six more months probation. I was told, "You should remember that date. It will be December 25, 2003."

Some time later the nursing home received a new administrator, so I called and asked to meet with her. She assured me that the two of us would meet without the social worker to discuss my case. I came armed with tapes, literature, and the works to find both her and the social worker ready for me. Each time I would begin a topic of discussion, the social worker would interrupt with such thing as, "You called your mom an SOB. It was witnessed." They took the tapes, and again I was not asked to present them to the staff. Yet, the social worker continued to tell me that the staff was afraid of me. Well, God help them if they ever get a TS victim as a client!

Eventually I did figure out why they thought I called Mom a fucking SOB. One day while talking to Mom, my tics were out of control, and her roommate who was very confused kept shouting, "Shut up! Shut up!" After a while I told her, "You shut up, you f---ing SOB!" I realize that this was a very inappropriate thing to say, but it was not said to Mom.

Chapter XVI

S everal weeks before Dad came home, I received a call from one of the town policemen informing me that the check for our water bill was returned because of insufficient funds. I immediately notified Teresa, who was acting power of attorney for our parents, and she said she would take care of it.

Dad thoroughly enjoyed recuperating in Teresa's home, delighting in getting more acquainted with his grandchildren, but when he finally arrived home that fall, he was very glad to get back to Coldwater. He again began his daily visits to the nursing home, but things never got back to normal. My visits were still limited to two days a week until Christmas Day of 2003 when I was at last allowed to return daily.

Christmas was very memorable that year. Teresa and her family were home, and that evening, with Mom holding one of her granddaughters on her lap and the other pushing her wheelchair, we all sang

Christmas carols. Everyone was more than surprised with Mom's ability to recall the words of nearly every song that we sang.

During the following week as New Year's Day approached, we visited and sang many of the old songs she knew as a child, such as Let Me Call You Sweetheart, Take Me Out to the Ball Game, etc. We spent many happy hours with Mom during those holidays.

In February she was again started on the medication, Depokate, and the following day seemed to be her old self when she stopped yelling and cursing. Dad thought that a miracle had occurred. Sadly, the recovery was short lived and she soon reverted back to her Alzheimer's behavior.

Mom had pneumonia several times that winter, and in March developed the inability to swallow even ground food. Eventually they had to insert a tube through her nose to her stomach to feed her. One day during the insertion of the tube, Mom began choking violently, causing Dad to call me to the nursing home immediately.

When I got there she was being suctioned, and the nurse said, "She's dying." I replied, "She can't be dying!" and began to sing her favorite songs to her. Miraculously she recovered enough to join in the singing, and they transported her by ambulance to the hospital's emergency room where they stabilized her and sent her back to the nursing home.

One Sunday in April she was again taken to the hospital, stabilized, started on an antibiotic, and sent back. That Monday Dr. Masser advised us to call Hospice to assist with her care. Dad called Teresa, and she came home that day. On Tuesday morning after Mass, I asked Father Dorn, our assistant priest, to give her the blessing of the sick. He also gave her what the Church called the apostolic pardon, freeing her from all her past sins and their punishments. He assured me that she would go straight to heaven. After all her suffering here on earth, I am sure that he was right. Later that week she became comatose, and on April 22 at 10:51 p.m. we watched while she took her last breath.

The funeral Mass was beautiful. It was sung by the Resurrection Choir with Sister Jane Francis and Ron Johnson, the organist, together singing the Ave Maria. As we followed the casket out of church, the choir sang On Eagles Wings. It was a very sad occasion, but I was at peace knowing that Mom was finally in her heavenly home, paving the way for us.

One thing that still upsets me is the fact that I missed visiting Mom for so many months. If I did not have TS, I would not have caused so much consternation with the nursing-home staff and could have spent more time just being with her. That time will never be returned to me.

We still find notes in the house from Mom saying that she had a good life, and would miss us very much. She also wrote that some day we would have no more adversities because we'll all be together again. Those notes have given me the hope that keeps me going. I also realized that getting back to work was the only way to retain my sanity and get me through the past events, so I returned the next day.

As if our lives weren't proceeding badly enough, we continued to get notices of insufficient funds in our checking, and due to circumstances beyond our control, suddenly found ourselves deep in debt. We had no money to buy food or pay our bills, and if it were not for my cousin, Sharon, I don't know what we would have done.

Shortly after my Aunt Mary's death, Sharon visited me, presenting me with a check for one-thousand dollars. When I objected to the extravagance of the gift, she said, "No, the money came from the sale of Mom's house, and you earned it. You helped care for Mom and visited her often. Keep that check for a rainy day when you really need to cash it."

I saved that money, and didn't tell my parents about its existence. When I retrieved it and presented it to Dad, there were tears in his eyes. We lived on that gift of money until Dad's retirement and my disability checks arrived.

Again we had to seek legal assistance, and with the cooperation of the bank, gradually started getting our monetary affairs settled. Everyone should have a Marlene Fisher on his side when confronted with large monetary problems. She has done everything to assist us, and we probably would have folded without her guidance. We were advised that it would take quite a few years to get out of debt, but with strict budgeting, we hoped to succeed.

I don't think that Dad will ever recover from that turn of events. He always prided himself on working hard to pay his bills, and was already very depressed over Mom's death. No medication seems to help him overcome his depression, and he can't stop blaming himself for the circumstances leading to his financial problems.

The only positive thing that occurred from this latest hardship was that Dad and I became closer than we ever had before. I think he finally realized that underneath all of my tics, OCD, and ADHD, a son with a brain existed. I became his power of attorney, and together we began working to become financially solvent.

Until we were the sole occupants of the house, I never fully realized that Dad has quite a problem with obsessive compulsion. When I was young, I remember his mopping the floors at home several times a week although they seemed cleaner than those in most homes. He also took much pride in keeping his place of work spotless. I thought it strange when people would stop to use the restrooms in his service station on their travels because they were so clean.

We are probably the best example of the "odd couple" that you will ever find. While my obsessions and compulsions consist mainly of obtrusive thoughts without a worry about how clean everything is, he is a perfectionist in being neat and orderly. I upset him by merely making a cup of coffee, spilling some of the contents when a tic jerks my hand, or leaving the newspaper on the table after reading it. The appearance of my room never reaches his standards so he seldom comes down into the basement. His last visit there resulted in my getting rid of all the "junk" I had accumulated over the past years. I'm sure that he has painted our outside fence six times this year because he wasn't satisfied with the color.

I think I could live with some of my problems if Dad only realized that I am trying my best to do things his way, but my mind does not always allow me to conform. Not long ago I neglected to ask him to get my medication from the pharmacy before he went to Celina. When he arrived home and found that I needed medication, he called me stupid and said some other hateful things. No apologies from me were accepted, so I retreated to the basement until he calmed down.

I continued to work for the bank as a courier, driving to nearby towns to make deliveries, and things were going fine until one day when I stopped at the pharmacy in Celina to get my medication. After completing my purchase, I got back into the car, drove away without stopping for the traffic light, and got hit by a large truck. Fortunately no one was hurt, and the officer on duty was Jim Stelzer, who was familiar with all my problems. By the time he arrived, I was in a state of panic, and he did everything to help me relax.

Considerable damage was done to the company car, so I feared that the job I loved was in jeopardy.

When my boss from the bank arrived, he assured me that my job was secure and I began to feel a little better. However I remained severely agitated about the entire episode and had to take some time off work. Several days later I was told that they felt it would be in the bank's best interest if I did not drive for them anymore, but could continue to work for them in the office. This was quite a shock to me, as I couldn't imagine working in an office and learning entirely new things. I felt certain that this was the beginning of the end of my association with the bank.

I discussed my dilemma with a number of my friends, and they all seemed to feel that their decision to stop my driving was a good one. They reminded me that with all the medication I was on and my fear of driving in bad weather, I was probably lucky to have escaped with a minor accident. They also thought that I was capable of learning another job, and should go for it.

In the back of my mind I was recalling the fate of John, whom we met when Dad and I went back to New York for a Tourette Syndrome meeting. John was born in 1962, a healthy boy who weighed 8 pounds and 6 ounces with no signs of any abnormalities. At the age of twelve, he was diagnosed with ADHD, and struggled in school. Not much later he developed symptoms of Tourette Syndrome, beginning with corprolalia and echolalia. He would grunt until his

145

throat was sore, and in spite of his discomfort, continue doing the same. He had difficulty concentrating, and when writing a paper, would erase its contents until the paper was full of holes. He also had severe uncontrolled spasms that led to much soreness in his neck and extremities. After a trial dosage of 8mg of Haldol made him unable to function, he was eventually put on 1 to 2 mg of the drug, with only slight relief from his symptoms.

At times he was isolated from his classmates by having to sit in the hallway during classes. On one occasion he was kept after school by the gym teacher five minutes for every tic he exhibited during his class. He was relentlessly mimicked by his classmates, and constantly received phone calls at night taunting him. His years in high school became only slightly better, and after graduation he was accepted into the school for practical nursing. After only a short time they tried to oust him from the program, but kept him on after his parents consulted an attorney. John graduated with honors and was immediately accepted into a registered nurse's program with the same results. Again they consulted an attorney and he was allowed to finish school, graduating with honors. He lost several jobs because of his symptoms, but they were never listed as the reason for his dismissal. He was last employed by the state of Ohio for ten years without any problems and was well liked by his fellow employees and physicians.

At the age of 40 he had to go on disability when his symptoms became worse following severe harassment from his supervisor, the hospital administrator, the director of nursing, and his nurse manager. Someone apparently was offended by his tics, etc., and reported him to the hospital board. He finally sought an employment attorney and filed suit in the U.S. Federal Court 6th district court against the State. John had affidavits from 12 fellow employees including doctors and won his case. The state appealed this decision, and two out of three judges ruled against him. His legal fees were over seventy-five thousand dollars.

Shortly before his 45th birthday, John moved into his own apartment. He became so worried that he would be evicted because of his outbursts, that he increased the amount of his medication. One morning after he didn't answer his phone, his parents found him dead. His death was ruled an accidental overdose of prescription medication. Another wasted mind from this abominable illness!

I accepted the new job although my hours were reduced, and it was quite an adjustment. Everyone was very patient with me while I was learning, and offered me encouragement even when I made ridiculous mistakes. Because of the pressures of learning, I became extremely concerned about the new procedures and my tics got worse. Although we kept the doors closed, it was disconcerting to my fellow workers whenever the "f" word escaped. One of the girls was especially offended and asked, "Can't you substitute something less offensive for that word?" I was determined to make a success of this job, so I brought in some literature about Tourette Syndrome, and gave it to the head of the department. She in turn must have presented it to the other employees, and they now have a better understanding of my disease..

Getting people to understand Tourette Syndrome has become one of my greatest goals in life. I'm reminded of an incident that happened after the article about Tom Noonan was printed in the Daily Standard newspaper. Shortly after its occurrence, I received a phone call from a lady in Celina. After she read the article, she became convinced that her son suffered from Tourette Syndrome and asked if I would mind talking with him. I immediately drove to their apartment and met Mike, who definitely met all the criteria for the illness. However, no amount of coercion could convince him to see a physician, so I advised his mother to keep trying to get him to seek help, and went home.

A few weeks later I received a call at 1:30 in the morning from Dru Kuenning who was in the emergency room with Mike. The other tenants in his apartment had called the police complaining about loud yelling, screaming, swearing, and guitar-playing coming from his apartment. After the police got there, Mike became very belligerent when they would not listen to his reason for this behavior, so they transported him to the hospital for evaluation.

When I arrived at the emergency room, they were making arrangements for his transfer to a psych ward in Lima, Ohio. After I explained to the doctor in charge that Mike did not need a psychiatrist but had Tourette Syndrome, he said, "What is that?" I said, "Look it up in your medical book, and you'll learn what it is." There were many people that learned about TS that night, and Mike finally agreed to see his family physician to get help. He always tells me that I saved his life.

Chapter XVII

One day last summer, I received a phone call from Gary. He had quit his position in the emergency room because of the immense responsibility of the job and joined a private group of doctors at the LaValle Metabolic Institute of Cincinnati whose specialty is "Wellness". They had done quite a bit of work with patients who presented many of my problems, and were having much success with their treatment. He called to offer his services to me free of charge. I did not have to stop any of the medication that I was presently taking, and he cleared the treatment with Dr. Masser. Although I was somewhat doubtful about it, I was also hopeful that maybe I would be rid of this horrible disease, at last, or relieved of many of the symptoms. Consequently, with the approval of Dr. Masser, I began a series of blood and urine tests and waited.

When the results finally arrived, we learned that I was deficient in numerous components, and would have to replenish them with vitamins, minerals, etc. Apparently these low levels were associated in part with the large amounts of drugs I had taken over the years and it would take a while to get the levels back to normal.

Soon a large package arrived containing my medication and I began my treatment. I was so hopeful that this would be the answer to my problems, and after a day or so I seemed to be feeling better. I began visualizing a normal life for myself and took my daily medications faithfully. Maybe my improvement was psychological, because after about a week, my symptoms returned and I was worse than I had been in years. Gary had never known me at my worst, so when I called him to report my progress, he told me that I had to be patient and give the medicine time to do its job.

By another week it was almost as if my body were again possessed by some demon. The tics were nearly as bad as they were before my diagnosis and the thoughts from my obsessive compulsion disorder were worse than ever. Because it was unbearable having no control over any of these symptoms, I discontinued the medications, again disappointing Gary and Dr. Masser.

After my body and mind returned to their normal state, I discussed the situation with Gary. He concluded that I had been placed on too much medication at the start, and recommended that we resume the regimen but on very low doses, gradually increasing the amounts as I could tolerate them. As much as I'd hoped for a positive outcome of this, I was afraid to take that chance again and begged off for the time being.

Recently Dr. Masser suggested that we try a new medication, so without blinking an eye, I exclaimed, "Why not!" After only a few days, I was doing much better. My obsessive compulsions were much less, and my tics somewhat subdued. This too was short-lived and all the symptoms returned in full force. We tried raising the dosage, and then lowering it to no avail. I think Dr. Masser felt as bad as I did, but we still had hope that something was out there that would overcome this disease.

For a while I attempted to use mind control to try to stop the coprolalia associated with TS, and began with the "n" word, that is seldom used in this area. Although I seemed to be making some progress with this, every step forward was followed by one backward.

I still miss my mother very much, but Dad has never accepted her death. He visits her grave every day, talking to her and making sure that the flowers placed there are in order. Often he returns several times in a day, and he does not feel that I pay her enough homage. I try to explain that we all mourn in different ways and my not visiting her grave daily does not mean that I honor or love her less.

Early last summer when Dad approached Mom's grave, he noticed a robin flying from the flowers on her tombstone. Upon investigation, he found a nest containing four eggs imbedded in the flowers. He was very excited about his discovery and told me about it as soon as he got home. We discussed the incident at length and became thoroughly convinced that this was a sign from God, letting us know that Mom is helping us on earth from her place in heaven. After that day we quietly closed the car door and approached the grave site with caution in case the mother bird was in the nest.

About a week later our area was hit by a storm accompanied with severe wind and rain during the night. Upon visiting Mom's grave the next day, we found that the flowers were no longer there, but about fifteen grave-sites away. What a relief to find the nest and its eggs were intact! We carried it back to Mom's monument, hoping that the robin's mother would return. Before long she was back tending her eggs, and one day while she was probably out searching for food, we found four baby birds in the nest.

One Sunday morning a short time later, just as Dad was backing his car out of the driveway, I spotted a bird behind the wheels and yelled for Dad to stop. It was a baby robin just beginning to try its wings for flight. To me that was one more sign from God that there would eventually be a new life for us all. Ever since Mom's death, I had been angry with God. I knew that she was in Heaven pleading for Him to release me from Tourette Syndrome, yet I was still plagued with the miserable disease. Since this bird business occurred, my faith was really strengthened and I became confident that some day there will be a resurrection and our family will again be reunited in paradise.

This renewal of my faith should have helped to improve my symptoms, but for some reason my tics got so bad by the end of the summer that I was afraid to go anywhere. I kept getting worse even after Dr. Masser tried to lower the dosages of my medication. The holidays were approaching and since I am usually very bad during that time, I became very worried. I was reminded of Mother Teresa who said, "I know God will not give me anything I can't handle. I just wish that he didn't trust me so much."

Toward the end of November Orrin called, and through our conversation, recognized the extent of my anxiety. When I told him the amount of medication I was on, he was amazed that I had not gone into liver failure from all the Haldol, Cogentin and Ativan I was taking. Some of my friends had said the same thing in the past whenever I took a few more pills to get me over a bad time. As a result of that phone call, Orrin called Dr. Masser, and they mapped out a plan of action. I was taking fairly large doses of Lexapro, Haldol, Cogentin, and Ativan, and with the guidance of Orrin, Dr. Masser, Dr. Brunn, and Gary I began to lower the dosages of those four medications. Before discontinuing Lexapro, I started taking Seratonin, following Gary's advice. I was warned that this would be a very tedious process that would take much patience. At about the same time, I became determined to stop smoking, and was started on Chantix for that miserable habit. To my surprise, my tics and obsessions began abating, and everyone noticed how much I had improved.

My next visit with Dr. Masser was a very happy one, as he immediately noticed the change in my demeanor. We hugged and he exclaimed, "It's a miracle!" The entire appointment was spent without the interruptions of my uttering the "f" word or picking at things. I began to think that maybe it was a miracle. Several weeks later I developed a cough, took some over the counter cough medicine, and found my tics and obsessions getting worse again. That experience finally taught me not to take any more unauthorized medications.

In early December our area was hit by a severe snow storm overnight, and I was supposed to work in the morning. Dad suggested that I call the bank and see if they were going to be open. I called and could hear someone in the background say, "I'll bet that's Frank saying that he can't make it here." I only live a couple blocks from the bank, and would have felt like a wimp staying home when everyone else made it into work. When I complained to Dad that my car was snowed in, and I had no transportation, he said, "You could walk."

Well, that wasn't what I had in mind, but I dressed in every bit of clothing that I could wear at one time and started on my journey. It was a beautiful morning! The only sound I could hear was that of my footsteps crunching on the snow, and I've never felt so at peace. With no interruptions from traffic or other people, I felt that I was alone with God and told Him that I knew Mom was in heaven where we would eventually be reunited. It seemed that God answered me and said that we would definitely be together again. I also talked to Mom, and she in turn reassured me. I wish I could fully convey the feeling I got from that walk but I can honestly say I have never been in such a state of serenity and doubt that it will ever happen again. When I arrived at the bank I received a standing ovation, and my day was complete.

The Christmas season was usually a time for me to go into a bad depression. In the past I decorated the house mainly to raise Dad's spirits, and it had become a chore to try to captivate the happiness that everyone else was feeling. Before the Christmas of 2009 I had significantly lowered the dosages of all my medications, and was feeling on top of the world. My obsessions and tics were nearly gone, and our home was decorated so much that Dad said we didn't need any additional lighting in the house. It's hard to describe how elated I was without the aggravation of all my symptoms, but I felt like a new person. My excitement was noticed throughout the community, causing some of them to wonder what I was using.

Shortly before Christmas arrived, our book was nearly completed, and we had decided on a publisher. I called Gary to notify him of my progress, both of the book and my improved life. Not too much later I received a home-made card from him that did more for me than all the pills on earth. The cover of the card contained a super hero with cape and all. It was entitled "Super Fu Fu Fu Friend." Inside the card was the following letter: "My Man !!! You are my super hero. You followed through on the task you set out to accomplish. You told your story for all the world to see and you did it with integrity and honesty. You have faced so much adversity in your life and yet you continue to battle back and show the inner strength that others fail to see in you. You my friend are a real man. You stand for your beliefs and do not speak with hollow words.

I am so proud to be able to call you my friend and honored to know you. You have added greatly to my life and to my understanding of the world through your generous sharing of your life. I was drawn to the spirit within you many years ago and now to sit and watch your triumph gives me chills. Congratulations on your journey.

Thank you Frank. It is a true privilege to know you. You have touched my life and now your story will touch countless others. I look forward to watching this grand parade, as your book becomes a reality. I love you buddy. Gary"

Several days later Marlene called from the bank, informing us that our loan was completely paid and we were debt free. She would not disclose the name of our benefactor, but that call made our Christmas complete. The generosity of all our friends was so overwhelming it's hard to put into words. We received enough money, gift certificates, etc. that our monetary worries were over for a while.

Recently I received a call from a friend whom I hadn't seen for some time. After we had talked for a while, she declared, "Frank, I can't believe that I'm having this conversation with the Frank that I know. I haven't heard the "f'" word, or bursts of tics once since we started, and it's just great!" Another old friend visited one evening, and we laughed and cried, reminiscing for several hours about our past experiences. It was such a relaxing time because of my ability to converse normally, and I hoped the evening would never end.

I can't help but wonder how long this relapse will last, but I've decided to live one day at a time, trusting in God that eventually a cure will be found for all victims of Tourette Syndrome, and we'll all be able to live normal lives. Until that happens, I thank the Lord for all the good things that I have achieved through this illness. Without it I would never have acquired all the friends that I have—-those who have accepted me for the person that I am, in spite of all my problems. I would not have been fully aware of how many people exist who use their abilities to make life better for others. Finally, even if a cure for TS is not found in my lifetime, I'm confident that my suffering will some day be rewarded in eternity.

Ending this book with the announcement of a cure for TS is not possible, but I am happy to say that much research has been done with some encouraging results. Recently Orrin called me with exciting news about a recent article in the New England Journal of Medicine. Several months ago the Yale School of Medicine's researchers identified a rare mutation in a gene that is required to produce histamine. This finding provides a new framework to understand many years of data on the role of histamine function in the brain and points to a potentially novel approach to the treatment of tics and Tourette syndrome. Past experiments by various labs show that mice with low levels of histamine are more prone to repetitive behaviors that are similar to human tics, and by increasing brain histamine, the problem is reversed.

In their recent study they discovered a family with a father and his eight children who were all diagnosed with TS. The father and two of the children also suffered from OCD. The mother and her family were all free of the disease. After taking DNA samples from each of them, they found that they all possessed a rare mutation in HDC (l-histidine carboxylase), a gene responsible for the manufacture of a protein necessary for the production of histamine to the brain. The rare mutation of this gene causes the protein to lose its function, depriving the brain of histamine. The findings of the mutated gene have resulted in several new medications being developed to increase the release of brain histamine, hopefully providing relief to many who suffer from TS and other related diseases.

This may or may not be the beginning of the answer we're all looking for, but we can be thankful that there are individuals who use their intelligence to give the rest of us hope.

About the Author

Frank Bonifas inherited Tourette Syndrome before the disease was recognized in the United States and spent a large part of his life not knowing why his violent tics, obsessions, and learning disabilities were present. He has written his story not only to spread the awareness of TS, but also to offer encouragement to anyone afflicted with it.

Frank is 56 years old and resides in Coldwater, Ohio.